West Nipissing Public Library

THE HANDBOOK OF
Canadian Log Building

Photo 1

THE HANDBOOK OF Canadian Log Building

F. Dan Milne

MUIR PUBLISHING COMPANY LIMITED
Gardenvale, Quebec, Canada

©1984 by F. Dan Milne. All rights reserved. No part of this book may be reproduced or transmitted in any form or by any means, electronic or mechanical, including photocopying, recording or by any information storage and retrieval system, without written permission of Muir Publishing Company Limited.

ISBN 0-919231-08-X

Illustrations by Ralph Ruppel.
Photography by John Patterson, except for front cover photo by Hisao Takahashi; photo 1, by Matao Ogata; photos 85-95, by Ryozaburo Miura; photos 3, 81, 82, 83A-1, 84B-C, 97, 99-103, 117, 119-122, 124-128 and back cover photos, by F. Dan Milne.

Muir Publishing Company Limited,
Gardenvale, Quebec, Canada H9X 1B0.

Manufactured in Canada.
Printed in Japan.

Contents

	Foreword	VII
	Introduction	VIII
	Glossary of Tools	XII
Chapter 1	**Placing Logs on the Building**	1
Chapter 2	**Footings and Foundations**	2
Chapter 3	**Log Floor Joists**	4
Chapter 4	**Framing the Main Floor**	26
Chapter 5	**Starting the First Round of Logs**	28
Chapter 6	**Scribing**	30
Chapter 7	**Settling**	58
Chapter 8	**Maximum Useage of Logs**	60
Chapter 9	**Roof Systems**	62
Chapter 10	**Window and Door Installation**	84
Chapter 11	**Partitions**	94
Chapter 12	**Cabinet Installation**	100
Chapter 13	**Chimneys**	104
Chapter 14	**Electrical Installation**	106
Chapter 15	**Plumbing Installation**	114
Chapter 16	**Stairs**	118
Chapter 17	**Screw Jacks**	122
Chapter 18	**Trimming the Log Ends**	126
Chapter 19	**Wood Preservation**	130
Chapter 20	**Timeless Love: Man's Attraction to Log Building**	136
	Glossary of Building Terms	141
	About the Author	146

Ann, this one's for you

Foreword

Over the years much has been written about the use of raw logs as a construction material. Many false notions on methods have been tossed about from one person or group to another. Indeed, many folks have embarked on a project with false information and false hopes only to realize too late they have made a serious mistake.

Log construction has been touted as the only way to build and even as an art form. It is neither of these and never will be. It is, however, a very real and viable alternative to the other forms of construction available today.

A cozy home built of logs, nestled in the countryside, is probably the ultimate dream of peace and solitude to countless thousands of people. If this home is constructed in whole or in part by those who are to live in it, then it has special significance. The feeling of contentment and satisfaction you get from acquiring new skills with the use of your hands has no parallel, and the tremendous sense of accomplishment when you can point at, and even walk through, what you have created is hard to relate.

If all people of the world could have the opportunities that some of us have, they too would choose to learn and take part in the construction of their own home.

Ed Campbell
Ed Campbell Log Buildings
Celista, B.C.

> Blank spaces adjoining the text and photo cutlines throughout the book have been left to provide space for translations into other languages or for making notes.

Introduction

The use of one of our greatest natural resources – logs – in the construction of homes and other buildings is an old form of building which has taken on new popularity in recent years. With this surge in popularity has come an inevitable landslide of "how-to" books, each claiming to teach the best methods and construction styles, and each designed for a varying range of building skills.

This book, **The Handbook of Canadian Log Building,** is designed for use by anyone in the log building industry: a once-in-a-lifetime builder, or the professional, hand-crafted log builder using these skills to earn a living. It is meant to be a reference book as well for building authorities and teaching institutions who must make it their business to become familiar with the latest techniques of the trade.

This book is the result of nearly a decade of experience by the author – a professional log building contractor, an instructor and a designer. The techniques involved, though, are the result of ideas gained from many sources, including students of the trade and other log builders. **The Handbook of Canadian Log Building** is designed to familiarize both the novice and the professional builder with as many pertinent techniques as possible, while

Introduction

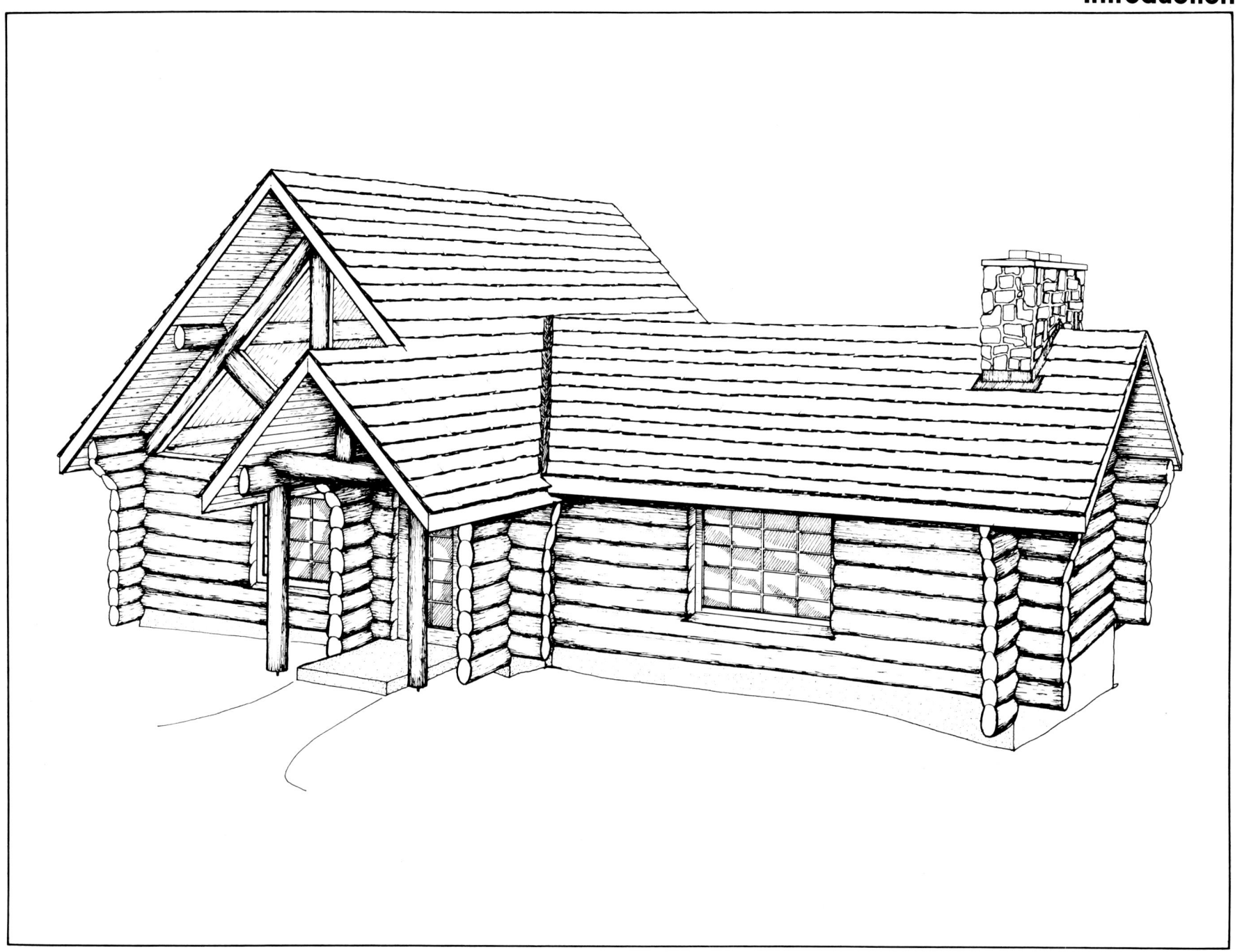

The Handbook of Canadian Log Building

keeping the importance of practicality in the forefront. This book won't, however, discuss such construction areas as carpentry, electrical wiring, masonry techniques, etc., because these categories fall into the realm of other specialized trades which are not the concern here. Readers requiring more information on these topics should consult local engineers, architects and building inspectors.

What this book is really all about is the basic step-by-step process of learning about log construction. Naturally, some of the steps may seem elementary at first, but it is advisable that the reader learn each step in order, and understand its total value. Once this understanding has been gained, short-cuts which will speed up the production process may occur and should certainly be followed. The intent here is merely to provide the best possible foundation on which to build. With this in mind, log building enthusiasts should read the book fully in order to realize that, in any building project, there are many ways to accomplish each facet of construction; with all the possible combinations available, extensive planning should be done before construction starts.

On a final note, remember that unlike any other form of construction, log building involves material that is in constant and uneven motion (causing settling) due to such occurrences as material shrinkage, material compression and differential

Introduction

loading of the walls because of roof design and roof loads.

   We don't want to "bog" the reader down with technical terms and data, but rather, illustrate as simply as possible the eventual outcome of each facet of the construction process. However, in order for the builder to achieve results comparable to the photos and illustrations in this book, he or she must have the willingness, desire and ability to work with their hands, handtools and a chainsaw. It is also of great importance that a natural love for wood and design be a part of the builder, in order that a beautiful piece of art be molded from the natural logs.

The Handbook of Canadian Log Building

Photo 2

Glossary of Tools

The intent of this text is to provide the builder with modern techniques of building, using modern tools. The idea of doing logwork in the 20th century by cleaning out our forefather's tool-chest is a misconception. During our ancestor's era, the variety of handtools available were a necessity, however, technology has provided us with an efficient array of tools. The builder need not feel handicapped without the old tools (though some are very useful for specific detailed work); beautiful building may be accomplished with the following set of 'Log Building Tools', which may be acquired through most hardware stores today:

1. chopping axe
2. peeling spud
3. drawknife
4. carving axe
5. carpenters square
6. canthook
7. water-bottle
8. staple gun
9. chalkline
10. scriber
11. safety helmet
12. hammer
13. chisel
14. tape measure
15. chainsaw
16. level
17. socket slick
18. handsaw

The Handbook of Canadian Log Building

Photo 3

CHAPTER 1

Placing Logs on the Building

It will be understood from the beginning that this is a textbook to aid the builder in practical methods of construction. In order for the builder to work in an effective manner, logs must be placed on the building efficiently. Whatever method used, whether it be a crane, a tractor/loader, a skyline or other, a rule of thumb is that if the time required to move the log from the deck to the building is longer than ten minutes, then the builder is working against an inefficient system and frustration will prevail.

Much can be said about lifting mechanisms, however it's the builder's duty to select the method best suited for him. The builder must also keep in mind that the type of construction that he is about to engage in, utilizes material that is perhaps 10-20 times his own weight and therefore requires practical and safe equipment to handle the material.

CHAPTER 2

Footings and Foundations

While foundations for log structures are very similar to those used with conventionally framed buildings, footings in general differ only in that they are increased in size for log buildings because of the weight factor. Builders should check with their local building inspectors or other authorities to verify the procedure used and to ensure that local statutes or ordinances will be followed.

There are generally two basic methods of building the foundation wall; *Fig. 1, the standard method for conventionally framed houses*, and *Fig. 2, the stepped foundation.* The latter involves somewhat more work, and in addition the builder must be careful to ensure that the basement has adequate headroom if this method is used.

Keep in mind also that in the first method a facia or trim board is needed to cover the exposed framing, while in the stepped foundation method the framing is entirely hidden within the concrete work.

Footings and Foundations

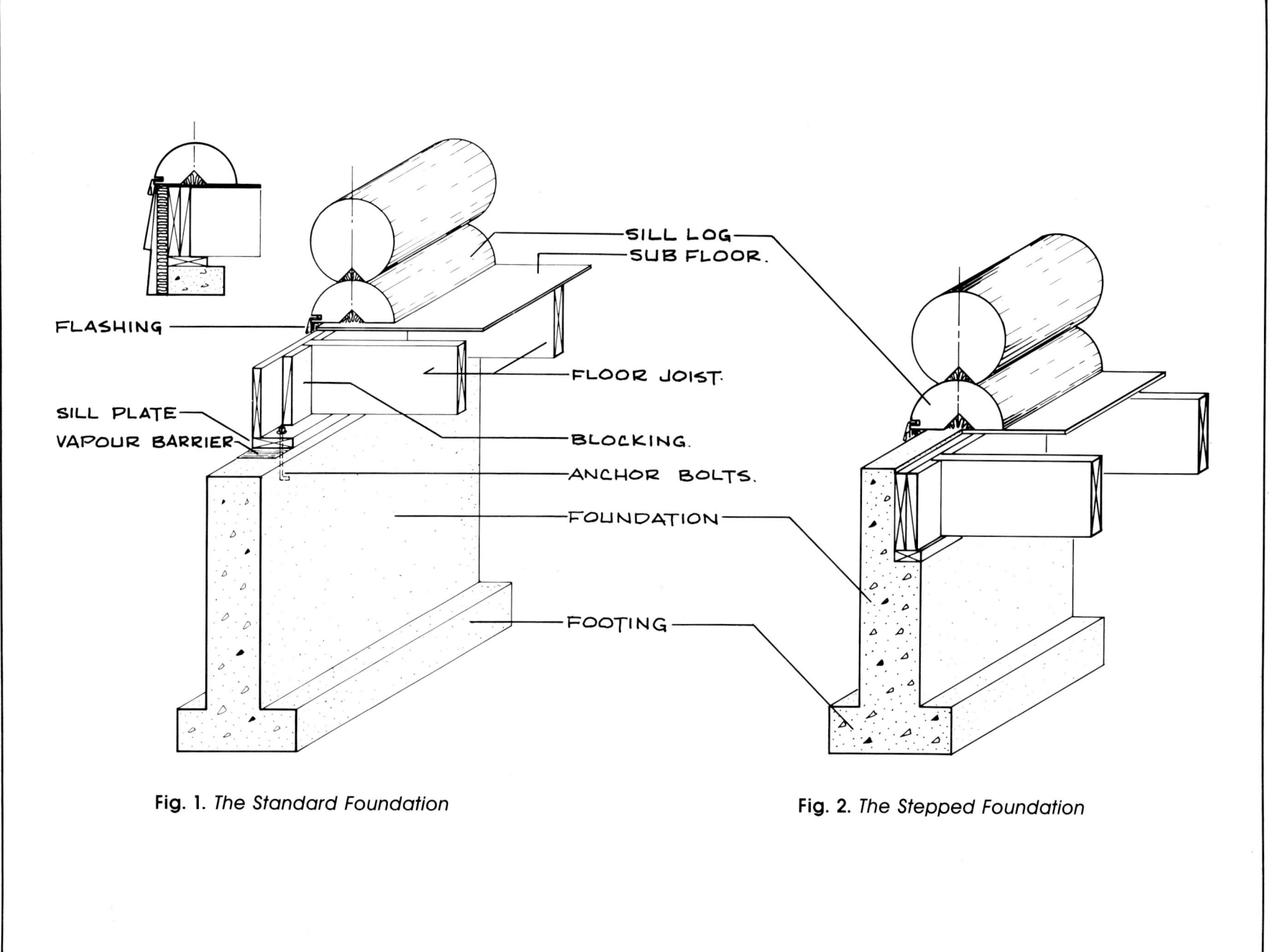

Fig. 1. *The Standard Foundation*

Fig. 2. *The Stepped Foundation*

CHAPTER 3

Log Floor Joists

It is probably best to use a conventional floor system when building a log structure, for the simple reason that if the basement is used for 'living space', then the floor joists allow the builder to easily conceal the electrical wiring, the plumbing pipes and the heating ducts in a very professional manner.

Builders should be aware of the use of log floor joists, because although not a widely used system for the main floor support, log joists are a common system for a loft or second storey floor support.

There are basically two widely used methods of installing log floor joists: **Fig. 3. The Tenon Joist**, and **Fig. 4**, involving the use of the **Double-Scribe Notch**.

The 'tenon joist' is used when a builder wants to terminate the end of the floor joist in the wall system, as in a common joist. If it is desirable to have the joist extend beyond the wall system for some aesthetic or structural purpose, such as a balcony, then the 'double-scribe notch' is the best method to follow. With this method, note that the portion of wood which remains in the center of the notch is normally removed with the standard 'round-notch'. The additional "webb" which is left lends a great deal of strength to the beam.

Log Floor Joists

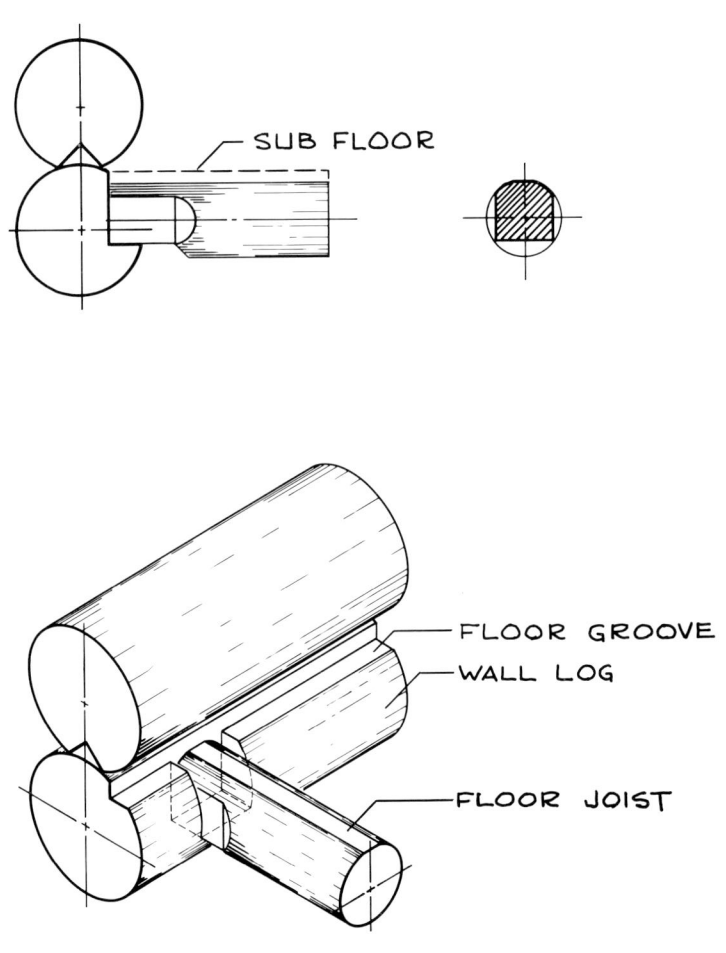

Fig. 3. *The Tenon Joist*

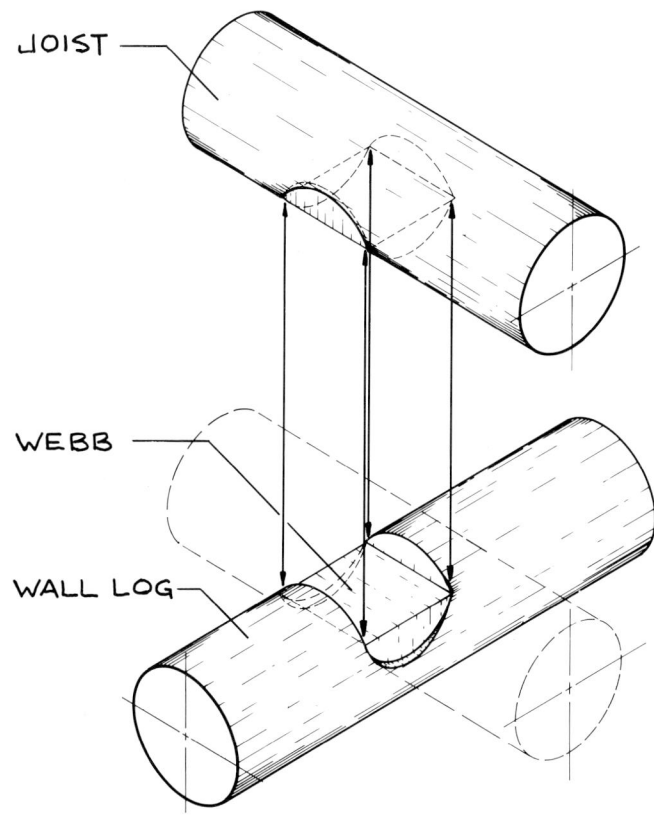

Fig. 4. *The Double-Scribe Notch*

The Handbook of Canadian Log Building

The sequence of steps involved in completing the 'tenon joist' is as follows:

STEP 1: Cut the log to about 2 inches (5 cm) longer than the final length of the joist.

STEP 2: Place the log on two skids (each skid having a small "v" cut in it).

STEP 3: Rotate the log so the "bow" of the log is in a downward position and block the log firmly. See Fig. 5.

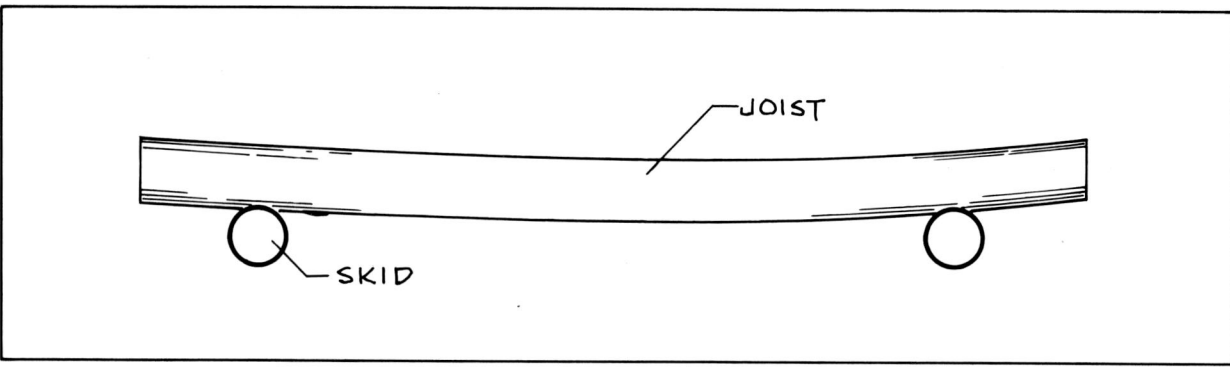

Fig. 5.

STEP 4: Trim the log ends to the exact length of the joist.

Log Floor Joists

STEP 5: *Place a 'Plumb Line' on each end of the log using a level*

Photo 4

STEP 6: *Once the size of the tenon has been calculated, layout on each end is completed using a tape measure and level. Note that the size of the tenon may not be contained within the perimeter of the log — this is a common situation.*

STEP 7: *Now chalklines are extended from end to end, connecting all corresponding points. It is important that the builder uses the point of intersection between the layout line on the end of the log and the outer surface of the log as the reference points.*

Photo 6

7

The Handbook of Canadian Log Building

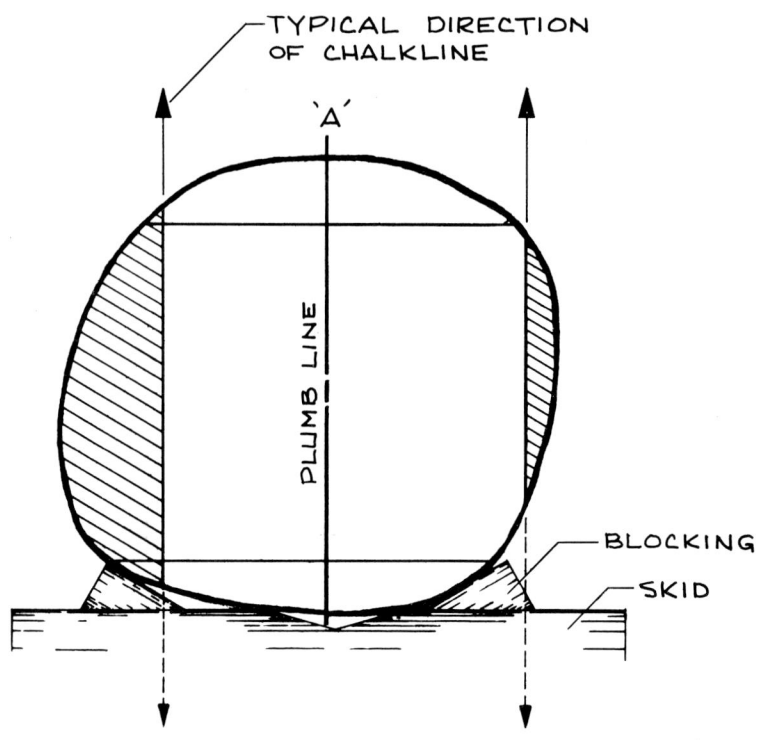

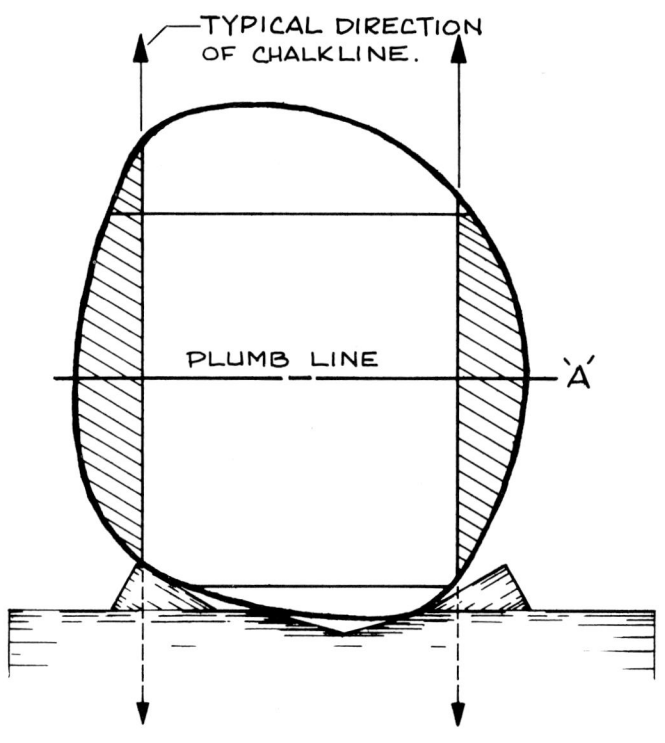

STEP 8: *It's extremely important that the builder realizes when the chalkline is 'snapped', it must always be snapped in the direction of the cut. In other words, when the chalkline is lifted, it is a vertical extension of the layout line. Absolutely no other direction is acceptable. Remember that these are irregular surfaces; this procedure must be followed accurately in order to achieve a perfect result.*

STEP 9: *Always use the chalkline in a vertical manner. In order to achieve accurate results, the horizontal lines must be rotated 90 degrees for chalklining. By using the PLUMB LINE as a reference, reposition the log and "snap" the lines VERTICALLY.*

Log Floor Joists

Photo 7

Photo 8

STEP 10: Once the chalklines are 'snapped', all that remains is to cut the two opposing lines with the chainsaw to the required distance, or the full length of the log, whichever the case may be.

STEP 11: Assuming a comfortable stance and holding the chainsaw in a horizontal position, start the cut into the end of the log at approximately 45 degrees to the end cut of the log because this keeps the chalk line and the plumb line in sight.

The Handbook of Canadian Log Building

Photo 9

STEP 12: *Once the cut is started, simply hold the near end of the chainsaw stationary, and pivot the far end of the saw, adhering to the chalkline.*

Photo 10

STEP 13: *Now by keeping the far end of the chainsaw stationary, pivot the near end of the saw, once again adhering to the chalkline.*

Photo 11

STEP 14: *Continue alternating this motion along the log.*

Log Floor Joists

Photo 12

STEP 15: *Correct procedure will guide the builder to the end of the log and very little touch-up work will be required.*

STEP 16: *Because of a pivoting motion, small 'ridges' will occur along the cut surface of the log.*

Photo 13

11

The Handbook of Canadian Log Building

Photo 14

STEP 17: *To smooth the surface, the use of a 'brushing' motion is used. Simply stand in one location (called Station A) and holding the chainsaw firmly, with the chainsaw bar at approximately 90 degrees to the cut surface, rotate the hips and shoulders to create a fan-type sweep across the surface of the log. This sweeping action will smooth the area marked in BLUE.*

Photo 15

STEP 18: *Now stepping sideways (to Station B), continue the 'brushing' in a similar fashion. This 'brushing' motion will smooth the area marked in RED. Note how the patterns overlap.*

Photo 16

STEP 19: *Move sideways (to Station C), continue the 'brushing' and smooth the area marked in BLUE. Again note how the patterns overlap.*

Log Floor Joists

Photo 17

STEP 20: *Again move sideways (to Station D), and continue 'brushing'; smoothing the area marked in RED. Note again the overlapping patterns.*

Photo 18

STEP 21: *Continue this action for the full length of the log.*

Photo 19

STEP 22: *The reason for the overlapping patterns is to ensure that if a trough is created by the chainsaw, the error won't become magnified by passing over it in the same direction; hence the direction must be changed for a smoothing effect.*

The Handbook of Canadian Log Building

Photo 20

STEP 23: *With the use of chalklines, the tenons are marked, cut and smoothed in the same manner as the full length cut. The back edge of the tenon is bevelled and dressed up with an axe.*

Photo 21

STEP 24: *The log joist is completed.*

Log Floor Joists

Photo 22

The Handbook of Canadian Log Building

TENON JOIST

Place log on "SKID". → Block the log with the "BOW DOWN". → Trim log to exact length. → Put "PLUMB LINE" on each end of log. → Complete all layout lines on both ends of log. → Chalkline, in a "VERTICAL" manner, all lines for cutting. → Reposition log to make cut horizontally. → Make cut using the recommended procedure. → Smooth cuts using the recommended procedure. → If there are no more surfaces to cut. → Finished.

If there are more surfaces to cut. → (loop back to Reposition log to make cut horizontally.)

16

Log Floor Joists

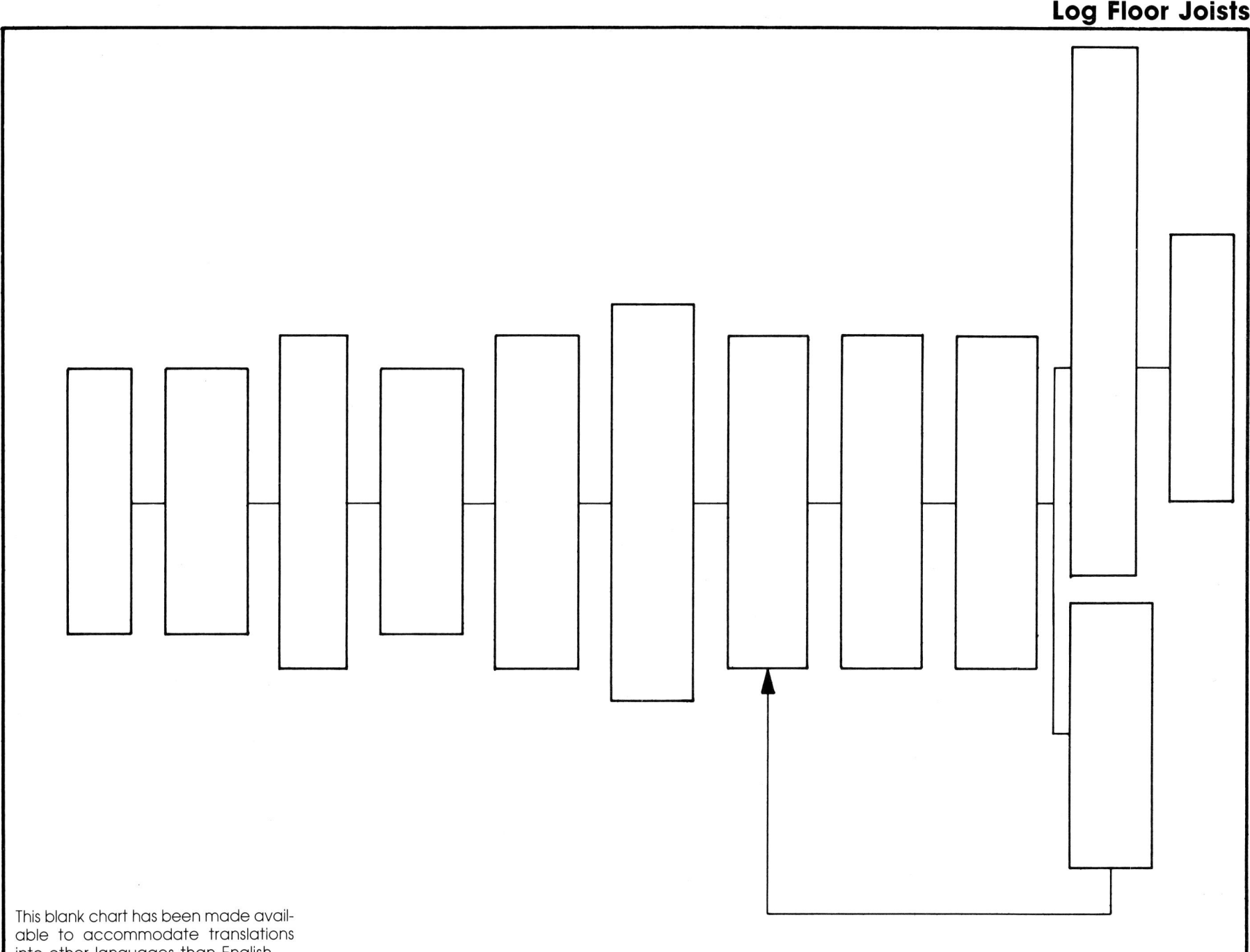

This blank chart has been made available to accommodate translations into other languages than English

The Handbook of Canadian Log Building

The sequence of steps involved in completing the 'Double-Scribe Notch' is as follows:

STEP 1: *Place the log joists over the wall logs as they will appear in their final position.*

STEP 2: *Block each log firmly with small wedges or 'log-dogs'.*

Log Floor Joists

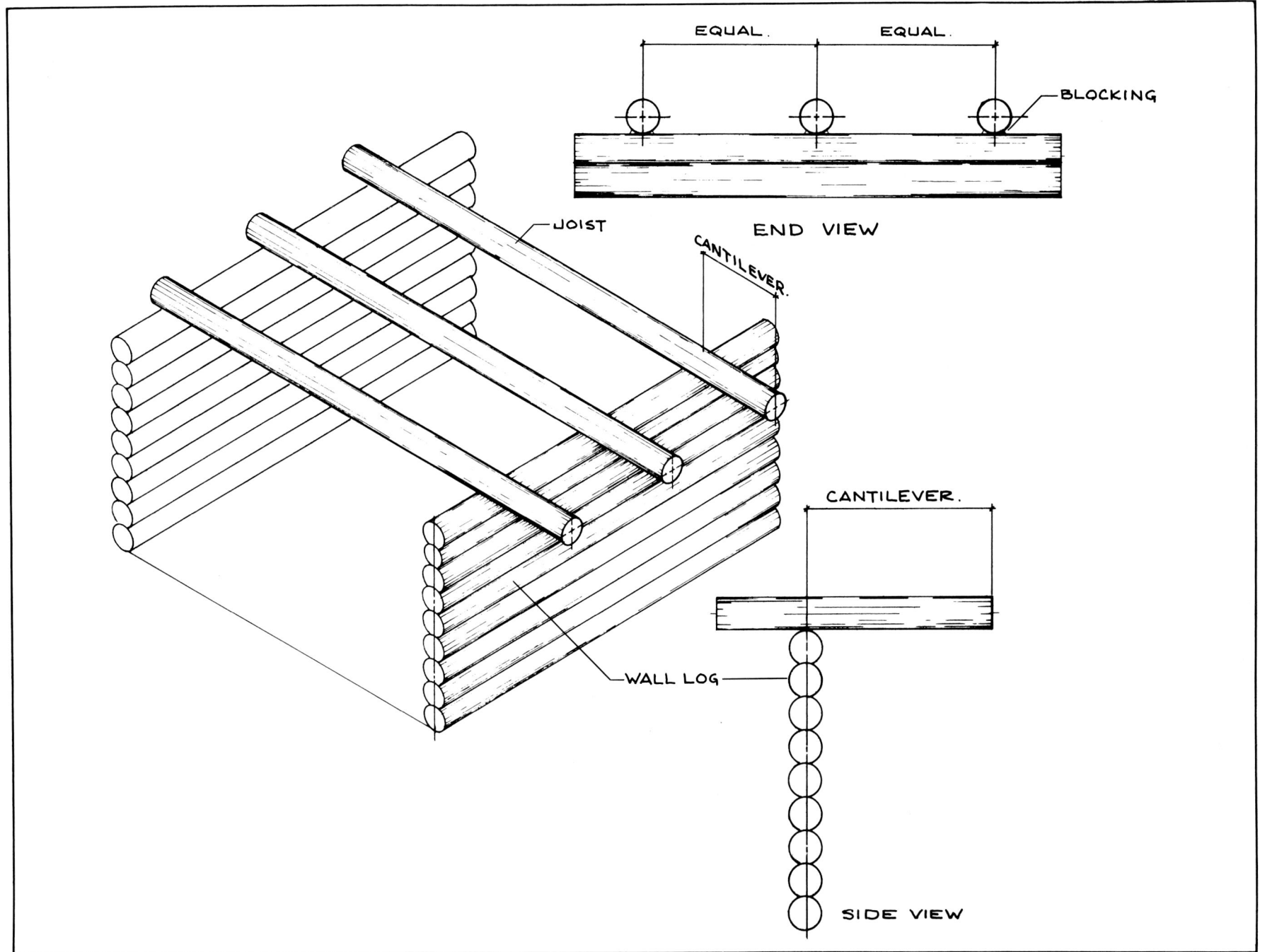

The Handbook of Canadian Log Building

Photo 23

STEP 3: *Choose the scribing distance, set the scribers using a PLUMB LINE, and scribe the notch for the floor joist as though it were a typical Round-Notch. Refer to Chapter 6 (page 31) and carefully follow the instructions for "setting" the scribers.*

Photo 24

STEP 4: *Now simply rotate the level attachment at the end of the scribers 180 degrees, set the scribers once again using a PLUMB LINE, and scribe the wall log with the same scribing distance.*

Log Floor Joists

Photo 25

STEP 5: *Choose where the level cuts will be as these will represent the surfaces inside the notch that will eventually mate together.*

Photo 26

STEP 6: *Where the level line intersects the joist scribe lines, two "critical points" are obtained. By touching these "critical points" with the leg of the scriber and positioning the scriber in a level position (using the dual level attachment on the end of the scriber), third and fourth "critical points" are located on the wall scribe line.*

STEP 7: *With the level, draw a level line through each of these points across the wall log to intersect the wall scribe line. Now two more "critical points" are located. With the scriber, transfer vertically, two more "critical points" to the joist scribe line.*

As a final check to ensure that the layout was done properly and carefully, the line connecting these final two "critical points" should be perfectly level.

The Handbook of Canadian Log Building

Photo 27

Photo 28

STEP 8: *The joist is rolled back.*

STEP 9: *The final layout is done by connecting all opposing "critical points" with a pencil line.*

STEP 10: *A flexible guide is a useful straight-edge for drawing the line.*

Photo 29

22

Log Floor Joists

Photo 31

STEP 11: *The cuts are done to remove all unnecessary wood.*

STEP 12: *If the layout and the cutting is done correctly, the final fit will appear to be exactly the same as that of a Round-Notch.*

Photo 30

23

The Handbook of Canadian Log Building

DOUBLE SCRIBE NOTCH

```
Block log in exact location.
        │
Place "PLUMB LINE" on ends of log.
        │
Select desired scribing distance.
        │
Set scribers using the recommended procedure for "ROUND NOTCH". ◄─────┐
        │                                                              │
Scribe the joist identical to that of the "ROUND NOTCH".               │
        │                                                              │
Rotate the scriber bubble 180 and scribe the wall log using the same scriber setting.
        │                                                              │
Draw a level line across the joist scribe line and locate "CRITICAL POINTS".
        │                                                              │
With a scriber, transfer vertically from these critical points and locate two more critical points.
        │                                                              │
With the level, draw a level line across the scribed wall notch through these critical points and establish two more critical points.
        │                                                              │
With the scriber, transfer vertically from these critical points and locate two more critical points.
        │                                                              │
Check with the level, these last two critical points should be perfectly level.
        │                                                              │
        ├──── If these two points are not perfectly level. ── Erase line. ──┘
        │
If these points are perfectly level.
        │
Roll log back.
        │
Connect the opposing critical points with a flexible straight edge.
        │
Cut the log, roll over and check fit.
        │
Finish.
```

24

Log Floor Joists

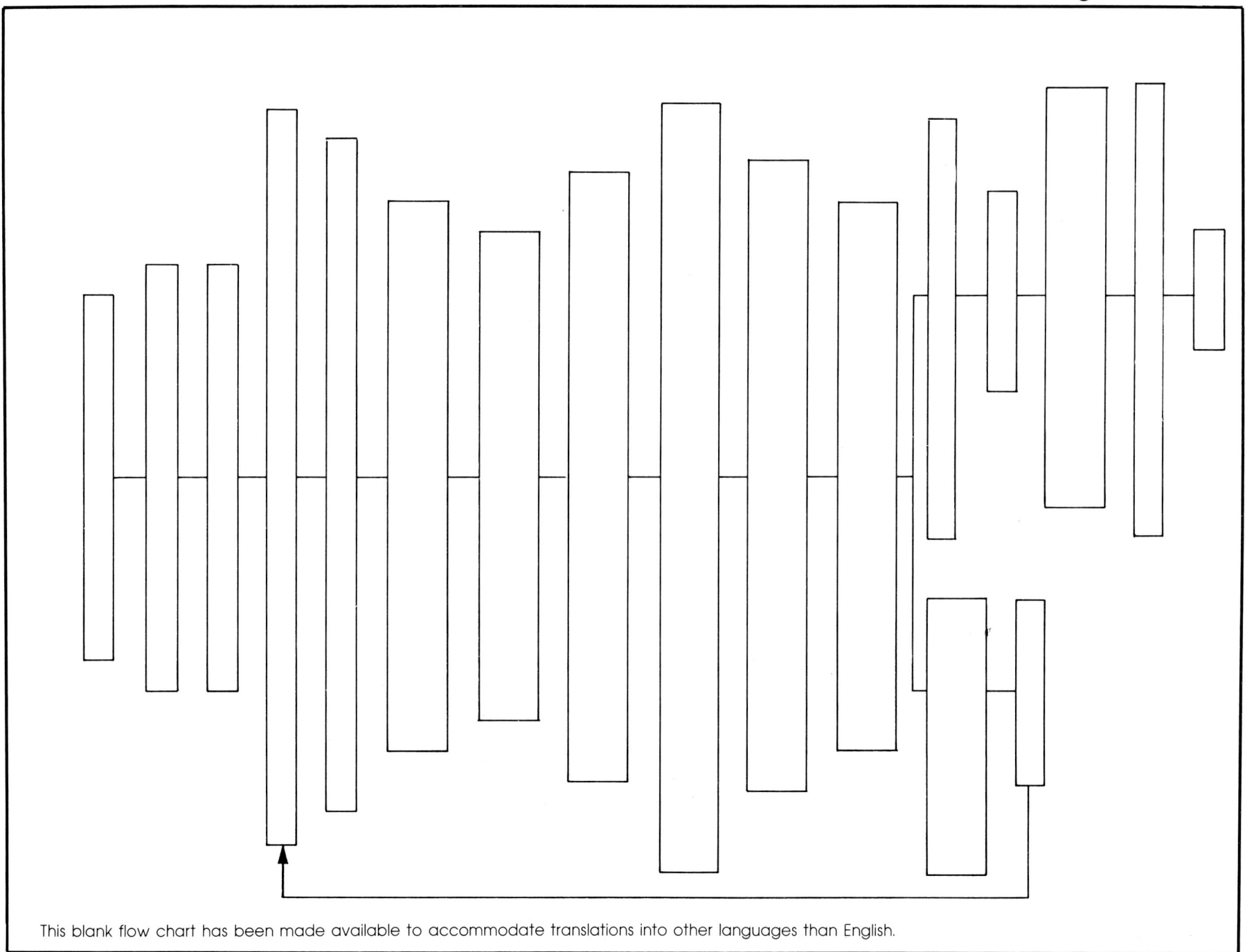

This blank flow chart has been made available to accommodate translations into other languages than English.

CHAPTER 4

Framing The Main Floor

Due to the considerable weight factor, the framing of the main floor of a log structure requires some knowledge of logwork. As discussed in Chapter 2, there are generally two standard procedures used to support the main structure: the standard foundation and the stepped foundation. In Fig. 7 (the standard foundation), the logs are bearing on the subfloor, which in turn is resting on the foundation. Here it is extremely important that additional blocking be placed, first between the floor joists to prevent the members from twisting sideways, and second, between the last two common joists at each end wall.

The reason for the second precaution is because the log on the end wall is bearing only on one joist and the plywood subfloor, and this is not adequate support.

In Fig. 8 (the stepped foundation), the logs are bearing on the concrete foundation as well as the floor framing, and so require very little reinforcing.

Framing the Main Floor

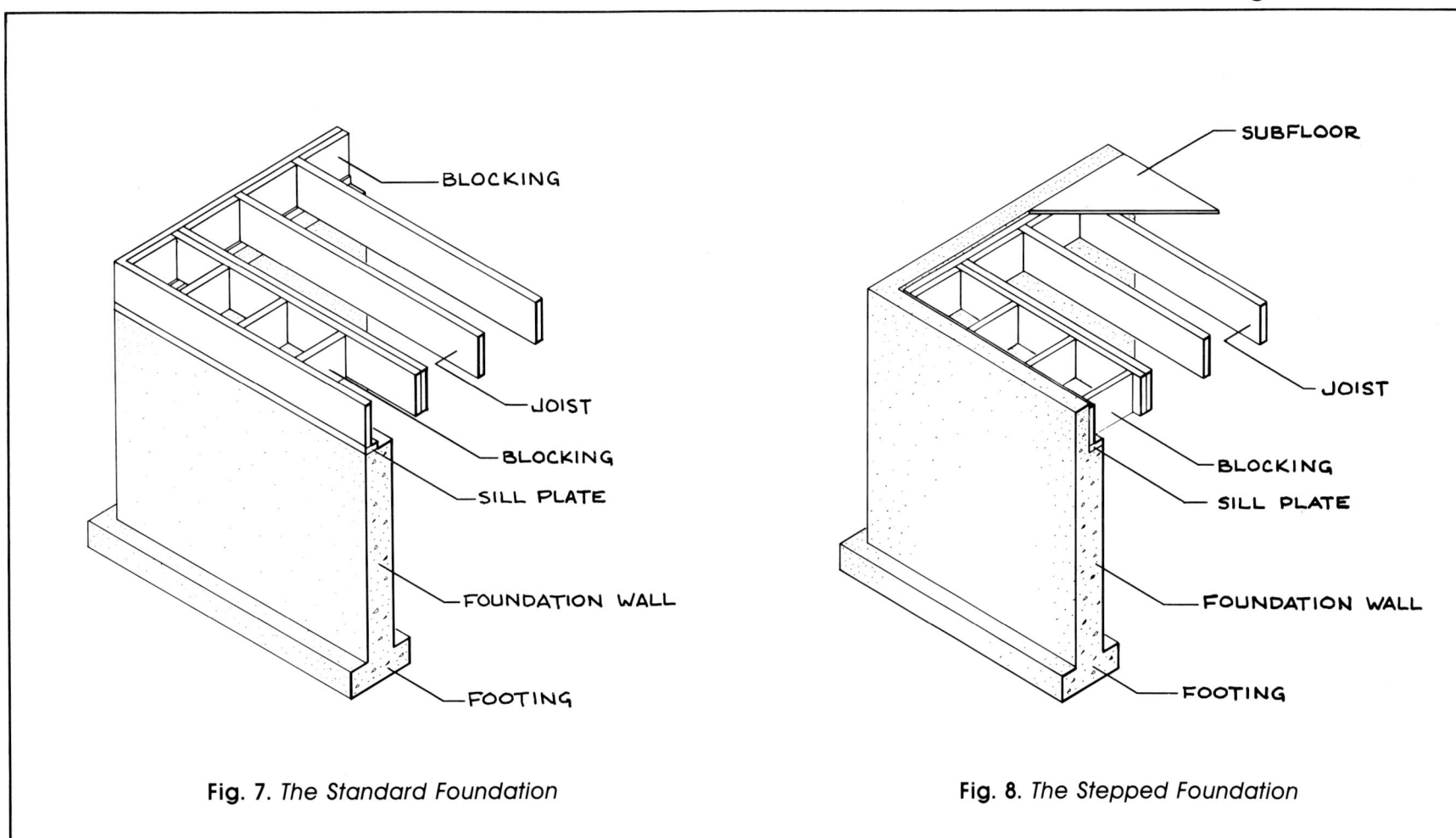

Fig. 7. *The Standard Foundation*

Fig. 8. *The Stepped Foundation*

CHAPTER 5

Starting the First Round of Logs

There are several options, as shown in this chapter, available to the builder when it comes time to lay the first round of logs.

In order to proceed with scribing, the builder must first choose which method to follow, and then proceed with the next chapter to fully understand the principles involved with scribing. It is essential to understand that each two parallel walls in the building must be approximately half a log higher or lower than their adjacent counterparts; this allows for a notch to be cut in each log, using about one-half of the log. In other words, the start of the building is with half-logs on two parallel walls. *See Figs. 9-11.*

For illustration purposes here, a simple rectangular building is used, but these basic instructions will apply even to more complex structures:

(1)   Split the first log in half, choosing either of the three examples illustrated on page 29.
(2)   Place the two half-logs on the sub-floor, with the log butts pointing in the same direction, clockwise or anti-clockwise.
(3)   Then place the full or whole logs on the adjacent walls, again with the butts pointing the same clockwise or anti-clockwise direction.

Now the builder is ready for scribing.

Starting the First Round of Logs

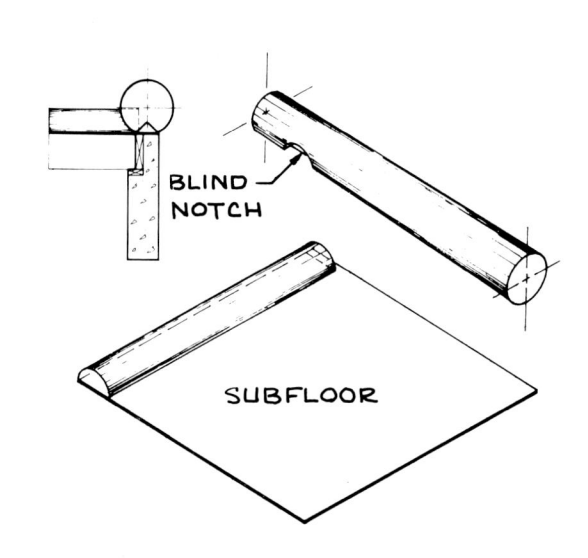

Fig. 9. *The Blind-Notch Method.*

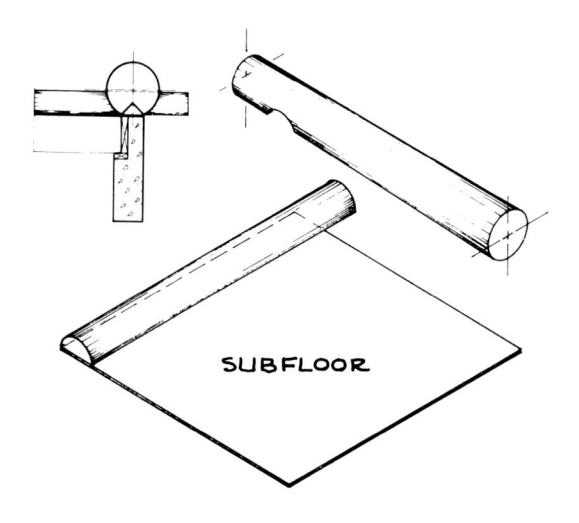

Fig. 10. *The Half-Log Method, Full Length.*

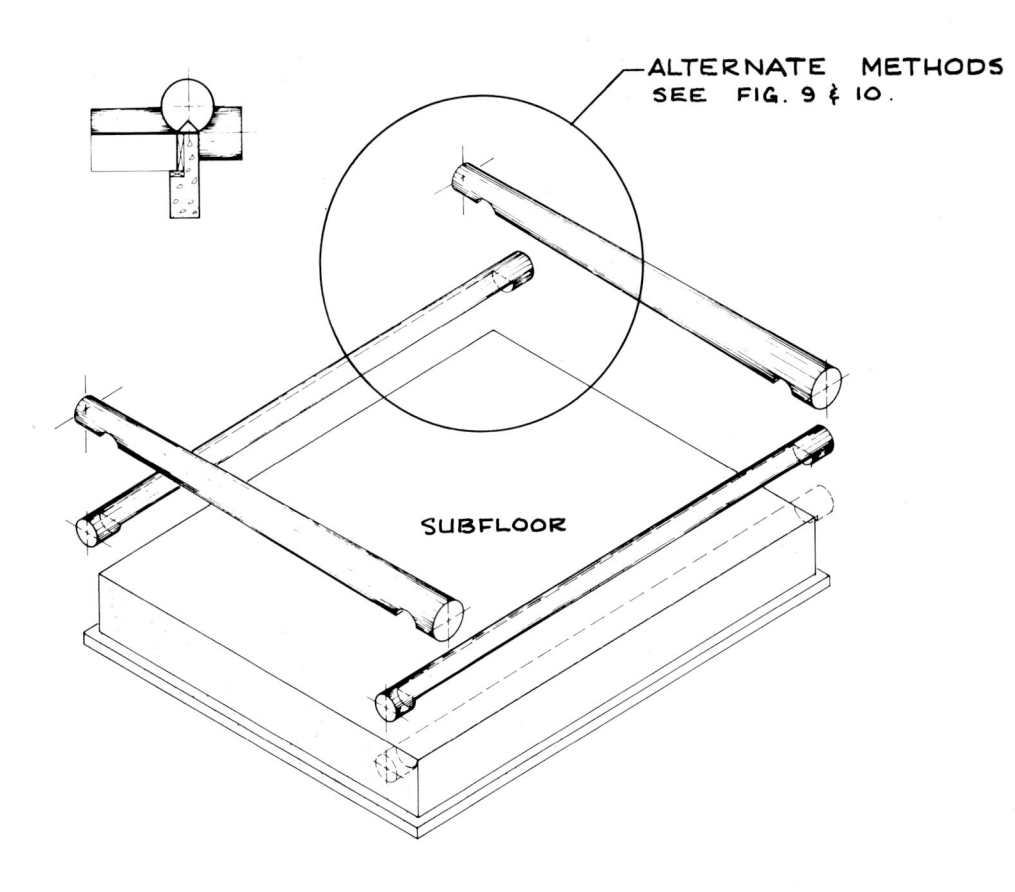

Fig. 11. *The Half-Log Method, With Full-Log Beyond The Notches.*

29

The Handbook of Canadian Log Building

Photo 32

Fig. 12. *A set of SCRIBERS.*

CHAPTER 6

Scribing

Scribing is, quite simply, the process of transferring the pattern of one piece of material to another, using a SCRIBER (see Fig. 12) to accurately transfer the pattern.

In logwork, builders are concerned with transferring the irregular pattern of the upper surface of the bottom log to the lower surface of the top log.

The following procedure is recommended. Remembering that we wish to work efficiently, the following sequence of steps is provided and the builder should study each step thoroughly and understand its purpose.

In doing ROUND-NOTCH CONSTRUCTION a two-stage process is followed. Stage one is the 'Rough-Notch' and stage two is the 'Finished-Notch'.

The Handbook of Canadian Log Building

Photo 33

THE ROUGH-NOTCH STAGE

The purpose of this stage is to work with the log and lower it to the log below with which it will be eventually mated. To accurately fit logs together, it has been discovered by the majority of reputable builders that the optimum finished scribing distance should be approximately 2 inches (5cm).

We are now ready to start logwork.

STEP 1: *Place the log on the building and position the BOW (or crown) of the log to the OUTSIDE of the building.*

Scribing

Photo 34

STEP 2: *On the INSIDE of each notch, measure the spacing between the two logs.*

STEP 3: *In this case the spacing is 6 inches (15 cm).*

STEP 4: *We now subtract 2 inches (5 cm) from this distance and our 'Rough-Notch' scribing distance is 4 inches (10 cm).*

Photo 35

Photo 36

33

The Handbook of Canadian Log Building

Photo 37

STEP 5: *The scribers are now set by placing the pencil and the scriber point against a PLUMB LINE.*

The PLUMB LINE is perfectly vertical in all planes. To achieve this, place a board against the building, making sure that it is perfectly PLUMB by holding a level against its surface. Nail the board solidly. Now place a vertical pencil line on the board, using a level. The line on the board is now perfectly plumb in all planes. By holding the pencil and the point of the scriber against this PLUMB LINE, adjust the dual bubble attachment at the end of the scriber to a PERFECTLY LEVEL POSITION. Now the builder is assured that when scribing the irregular surfaces of the logs to one another, that the eventual contact surfaces will be directly in line – one above the other.

Scribing

Photo 38

STEP 6: *Scribe the notch which the scriber is now set for. Always scribe a notch FROM THE BOTTOM — TOWARDS THE TOP.*

STEP 7: *Repeat STEPS 2 — 6 for every other notch on the log.*

35

The Handbook of Canadian Log Building

Photo 39

Photo 40

Photo 41

STEP 8: *Roll the log back, toward the inside of the building and make a vertical cut from the top of the log downward to the scribe line.*

STEP 9: *From the top of the log, where the scribe line curves to the opposite side, start a diagonal cut towards the bottom of the notch. Ideally, the end of this cut should be approximately 1 inch (2.5 cm) from the initial cut.*

STEP 10: *Repeat STEP 9 for the other segment of the notch.*

Scribing

Photo 42

Photo 43

Photo 44

STEP 13: *By crossing over the stepped cuts, the builder now smooths the notch.*

STEP 11: *With an axe, remove the two wedge-shaped pieces of wood. Smooth the bottom of the notch with a 'brushing motion'. Note that the chainsaw bar crosses over the original cuts.*

STEP 12: *By using the full length of the chainsaw bar, a series of cuts are made, originating at or near the upper part of the notch, downward toward the centre. Note that the amount of wood removed by each cut is exactly the thickness of the saw kerf.*

The Handbook of Canadian Log Building

Photo 45

STEP 15: *Repeat STEPS 12 — 14 for the other segment of the notch.*

STEP 14: *Work in a safe, comfortable position always adhering to the scribe line.*

Scribing

Photo 46

STEP 16: *The 'Rough-Notch' is now complete and ready for fitting to the log below. Note that the scribe line is visible around the notch. Repeat STEPS 8 — 14 for every other notch on the log.*

The Handbook of Canadian Log Building

Photo 47

STEP 17: *Above each notch, the shoulders of the log are dressed with an axe. This will prevent any 'recurve situation'* (see glossary of Building Terms).

STEP 18: *The finished 'dressed shoulder'. Repeat STEP 17 for every other notch on the log.*

Photo 48

40

Scribing

Photo 49

STEP 20: *When beginning to do logwork, re-scribing the notches to achieve this parallel distance is common practice. The builder need not feel embarrassed and think that this is a result of poor workmanship, because many factors can cause STEP 19 to occur. Time is well spent if the builder re-scribes and achieves a parallel spacing rather than omitting this procedure.*

STEP 19: *We now check that there is a parallel space between the two logs. If the space is not parallel, re-scribe one of the notches using the procedures outlined in STEPS 2 — 6 and remove the necessary wood.*

The Handbook of Canadian Log Building

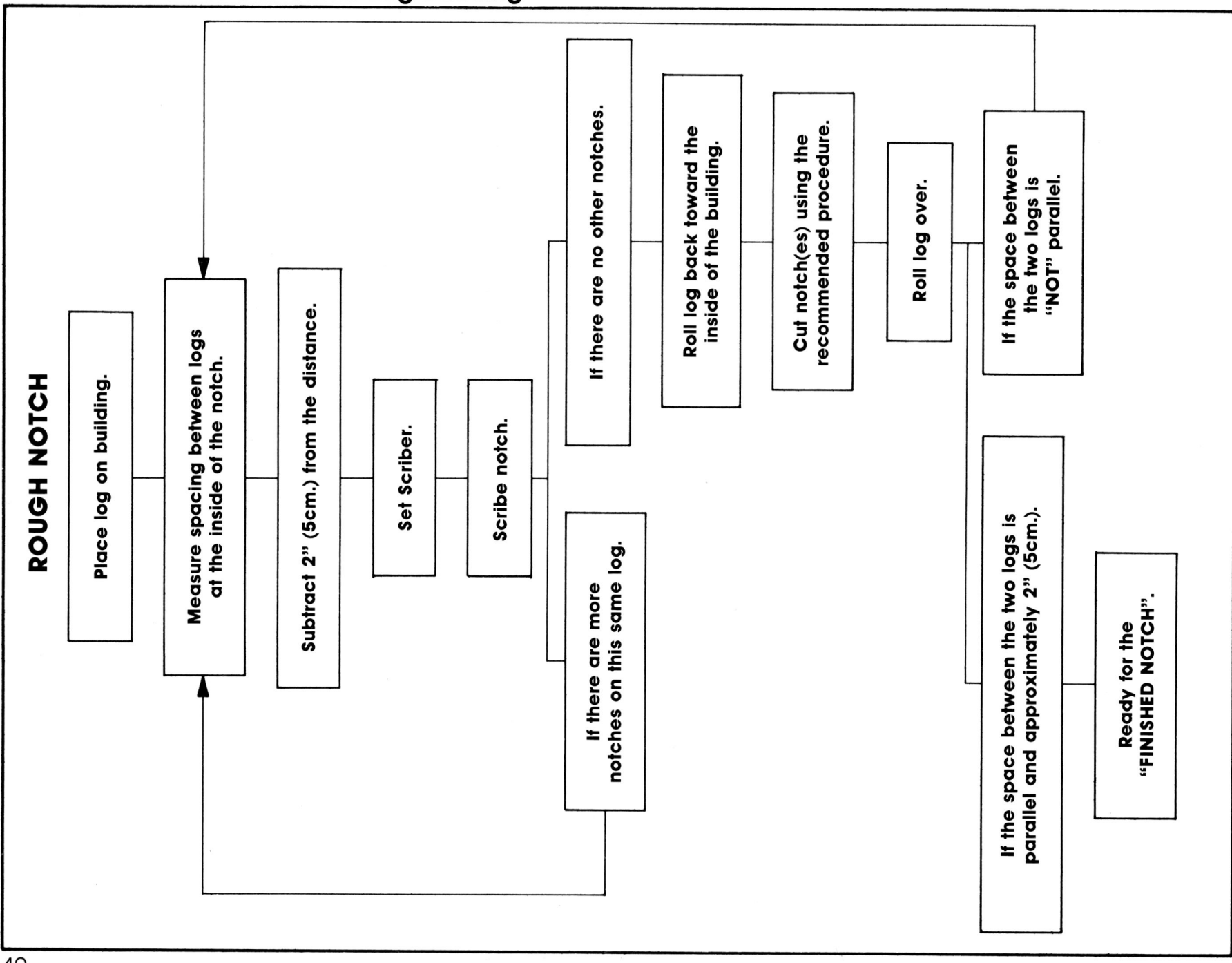

ROUGH NOTCH

Place log on building. → Measure spacing between logs at the inside of the notch. → Subtract 2" (5cm.) from the distance. → Set Scriber. → Scribe notch.

From Scribe notch:
- If there are more notches on this same log. → (return to Measure spacing between logs at the inside of the notch.)
- If there are no other notches. → Roll log back toward the inside of the building. → Cut notch(es) using the recommended procedure. → Roll log over.
  - If the space between the two logs is "NOT" parallel. → (return to Place log on building.)
  - If the space between the two logs is parallel and approximately 2" (5cm.). → Ready for the "FINISHED NOTCH".

42

Scribing

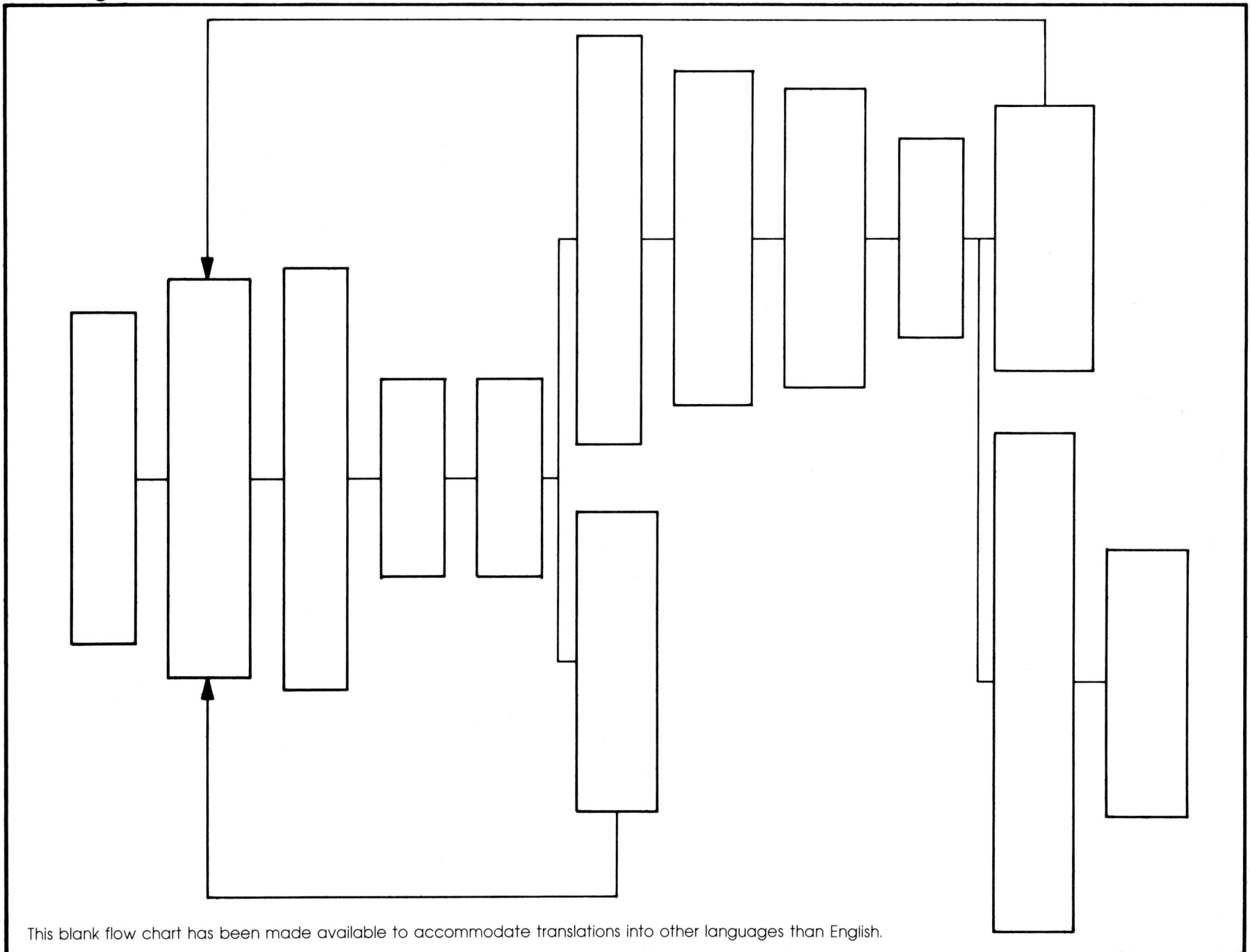

This blank flow chart has been made available to accommodate translations into other languages than English.

43

The Handbook of Canadian Log Building

THE FINISHED-NOTCH STAGE

If the 'Rough-Notch' stage was followed correctly, then the space between the two logs should now be approximately 2 inches (5 cm).

A great deal of care must be taken now to fit the logs.

Photo 50

STEP 1: *With a level, mark each end of the log for its trimming length.*

Scribing

Photo 51

STEP 2: *It's good practice to also sight to an opposing corner to get an accurate cutting line on the log.*

Photo 52

STEP 3: *Again, using an opposite corner as a sighting object, aim the bar of the chainsaw and concentrate on following the cut line.*

Photo 53

STEP 4: *Once the ends are trimmed and the log is placed DIRECTLY above its final resting position, a 'Plumb Line' is put on the end of the log. By using the 'Plumb Line' on the preceding round as a guide, a line is placed on the working log with a level.*

The Handbook of Canadian Log Building

Photo 54

STEP 5: By viewing the space between the logs, we now locate the "widest distance". It is *not* necessary to check between the logs beyond the notches (ie. the overhang).

Photo 55

STEP 6: Once the "widest distance" has been found, we add 1/4 inch (6 mm) to this setting. This additional amount determines the width of the lateral groove at this, the widest, scribing space. Since the space between the logs is closer at every other point along the scribing path, the width of the lateral groove will be wider than at the point of the original scriber setting.

STEP 7: The scriber is now set with the pencil and the scriber points each placed against the PLUMB LINE. This is the same PLUMB LINE used when setting the scribers during the 'Rough-Notch' stage. The dual bubble attachment is set in a perfect level position. When scribing, the builder is now assured that the irregular surfaces when scribed to one another will eventually mate together because the direct line of scribing has corresponding points directly above each other.

Photo 56

46

Scribing

Photo 57

STEP 8: *Scribe the notch,* always *keeping the dual level bubbles PERFECTLY LEVEL.*

Photo 58

STEP 9: *Scribe the lateral groove,* always *keeping the dual level bubbles PERFECTLY LEVEL.*

Photo 59

STEP 10: *Scribe the end cove,* always *keeping the dual level bubbles PERFECTLY LEVEL.*

The Handbook of Canadian Log Building

Photo 60

STEP 11: *Roll the log back, towards the inside of the building, to avoid the possibility of the log rolling off the building and injuring the builder. Check to make sure that there is a CONTINUOUS scribe line. If this is not the case, return the log to its scribing location (by re-aligning the log using the PLUMB LINES) and re-scribe the log.*

Photo 61

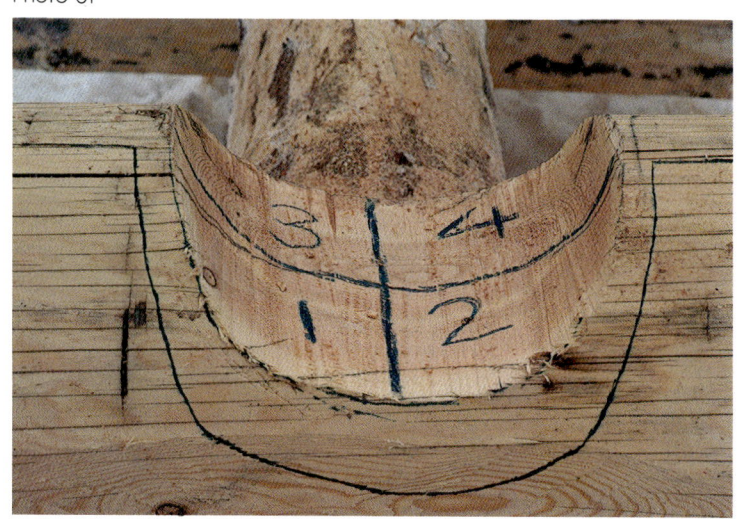

STEP 12: *The notch will now be worked in four segments.*

Photo 62

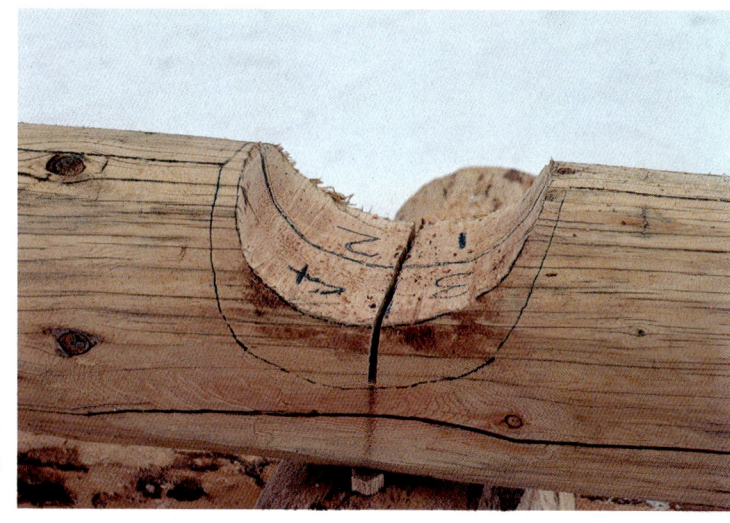

STEP 13: *An initial vertical cut is made at the bottom of the notch. The cut should be about 1/2 inch (12 mm) from the scribe line.*

48

Scribing

Photo 63

STEP 14: *Quadrant #1 is removed by first cutting a small "v".*

Photo 64

STEP 15: *A series of stepped cuts, similar to the 'Rough-Notch' procedure, are made. ALWAYS keep approximately 1/2 inch (12 mm) away from the scribe line.*

Photo 65

STEP 16: *Remove Quadrant #2 in a similar fashion, always working from the near side of the log.*

49

The Handbook of Canadian Log Building

Photo 66

STEP 17: Quadrant #3 is removed in a similar manner, however move to the other side of the log so that once again the builder may work from the near side of the notch.

Photo 67

STEP 18: *Remove Quadrant #4.*

Photo 68

STEP 19: *With a chisel, remove the outer shell of wood around the notch. This will eliminate any splintering of the wood fibers at the notch when working close to the scribe line with the chainsaw.*

Scribing

Photo 69

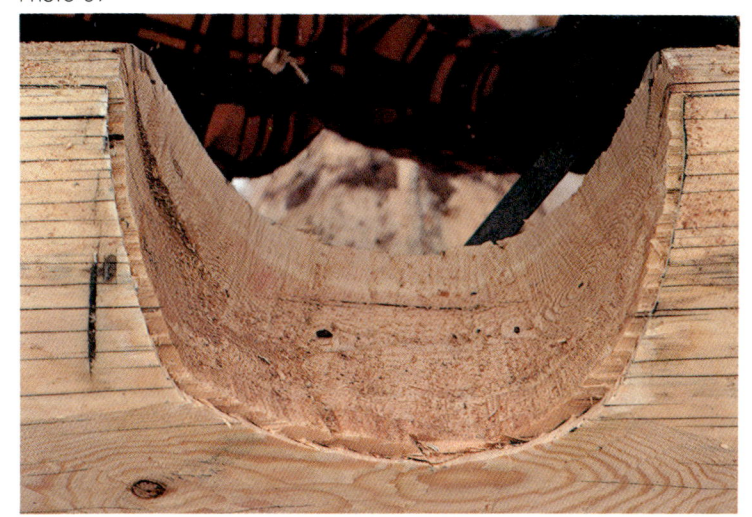

Photo 70

STEP 20: Continue all around the notch and do both sides.

STEP 21: Using the chainsaw, remove the centrewood of the notch. Work one half of the notch from the near side, then move to the opposite side and finish the notch. The finished notch should be slightly concave (about 1/2 inch or 12 mm) for insulating purposes.

Photo 71

STEP 22: The outer 'cove' is accomplished by first cutting a small "v", then scooping the final section with the chainsaw.

51

The Handbook of Canadian Log Building

Photo 72

Photo 73

Photo 74

STEP 23: *With the log in a vertical position (note the 'Plumb Line'), a shallow saw-cut of about 1 inch (2.5 cm) is made along the waste side of the lateral scribe line.*

STEP 24: *By rotating the log (note the 'Plumb Line'), and using the initial saw cut as a guide line, the lateral cut is made along the length of the log.*

STEP 25: *By rotating the log in the opposite direction (note the 'Plumb Line'), again using the initial cut as a guide, the lateral cut is completed.*

Scribing

Photo 75

Photo 76

Photo 77

STEP 26: *The LATERAL GROOVE is completed and final touch-up may be done with either an axe, chisel or slick.*

STEP 27: *Once the log has been correctly fitted, insulation is stapled in the notch and along the lateral groove.* (At the time of this publication, materials other than fibreglass are being experimented with and the reader may wish to choose an alternate insulating material).

STEP 28: *The entire log, from notch-to-notch, is insulated.*

53

The Handbook of Canadian Log Building

Photo 78

STEP 29: *The log is rolled back and re-aligned, using the 'Plumb Line' as the reference mark.*

Photo 79

STEP 30: *Hardwood wedges are driven into the upper surfaces of the log approximately every 24 inches (62 cm). This is to pre-stress the log and localize the checking to the top surface of the log.*

Photo 80

STEP 31: *The wedges are trimmed.*

Scribing

Photo 81

Continue with all the wall logs by alternating the butt/top directions on succeeding rounds.

The Handbook of Canadian Log Building

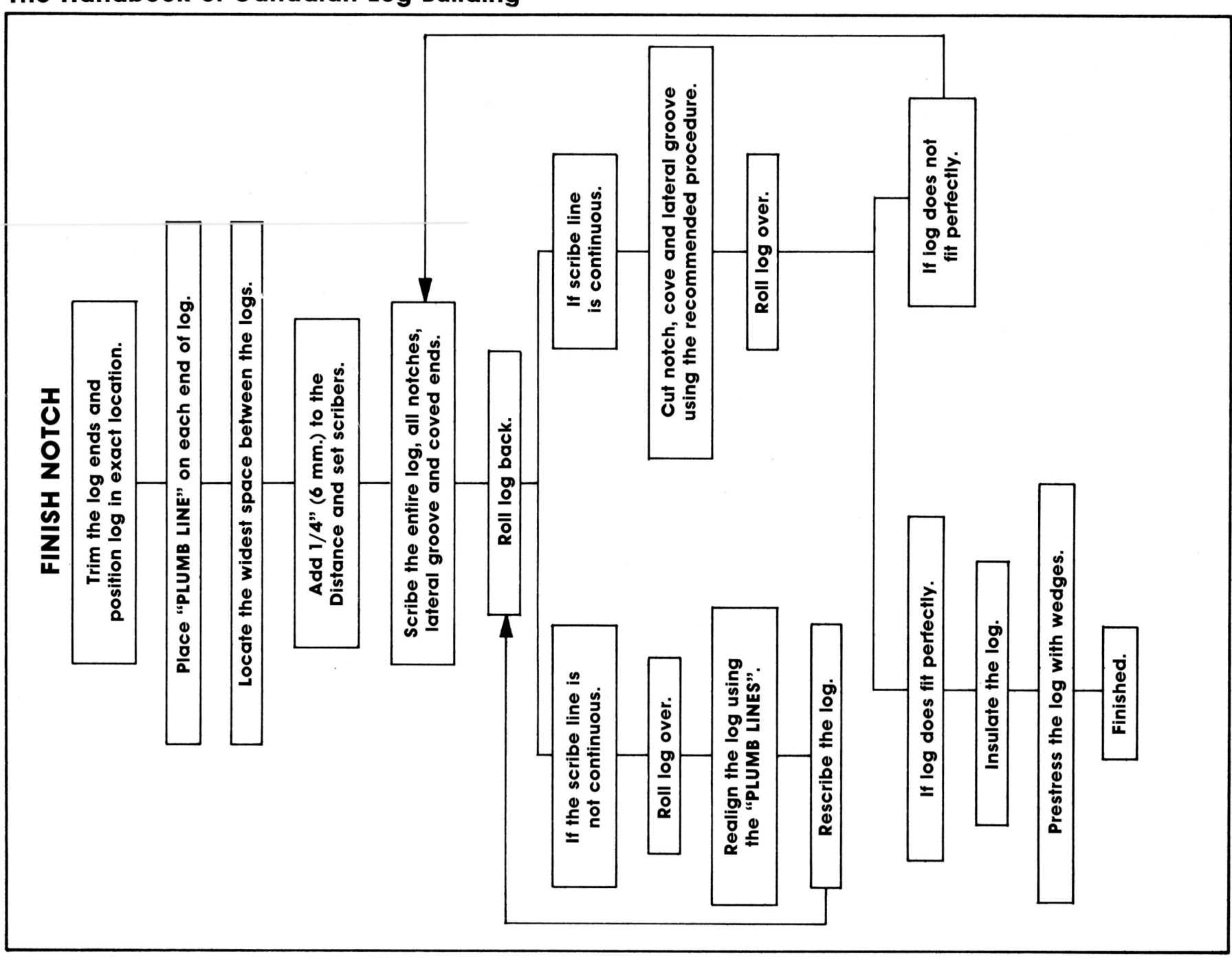

FINISH NOTCH

```
Trim the log ends and position log in exact location.
  → Place "PLUMB LINE" on each end of log.
  → Locate the widest space between the logs.
  → Add 1/4" (6 mm.) to the Distance and set scribers.
  → Scribe the entire log, all notches, lateral groove and coved ends.
  → Roll log back.
      ├─ If scribe line is continuous.
      │    → Cut notch, cove and lateral groove using the recommended procedure.
      │    → Roll log over.
      │        ├─ If log does not fit perfectly. → (back to Scribe the entire log)
      │        └─ If log does fit perfectly.
      │             → Insulate the log.
      │             → Prestress the log with wedges.
      │             → Finished.
      └─ If the scribe line is not continuous.
           → Roll log over.
           → Realign the log using the "PLUMB LINES".
           → Rescribe the log.
           → (back to Roll log back)
```

56

Scribing

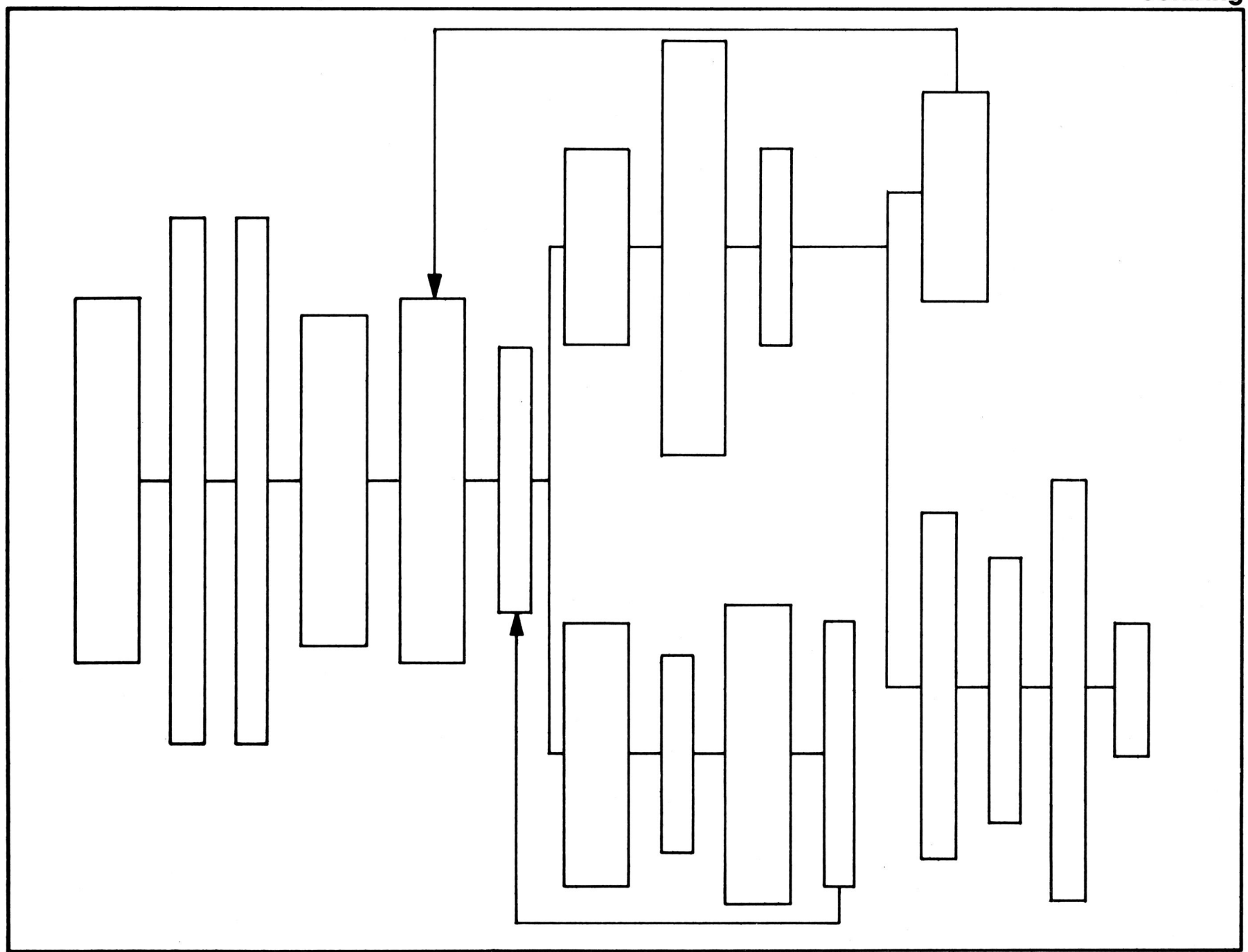

This blank flow chart has been made available to accommodate translation into languages other than English.

CHAPTER 7

Settling

Settling, one of the most important factors to keep in mind at all times when engaged in either designing or building a log structure, is a result of two things:

(1) the natural shrinkage of the wood, and
(2) the compression of the wood fibres as one log rests on another. It's important for the builder to remember that logs shrink diametrically and the amount of shrinkage longitudinally is negligible.

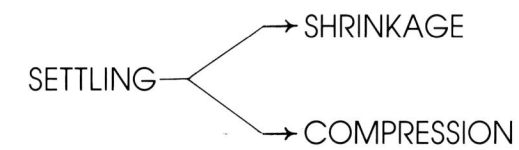

```
                    → SHRINKAGE
    SETTLING ──┤
                    → COMPRESSION
```

So each factor is considered equally for all calculations, the builder should assume 50 per cent of all settling is due to shrinkage, while the other 50 per cent is caused by compression.

Builders always use two calculations to arrive at the proper settling allowance. The reason for this duality depends mostly on the size of material used. Once the calculations are made, always assume the greater of the two values for the settling allowance.

The Formulas are on the facing page.

Settling

FORMULAS FOR CALCULATING SETTLING ALLOWANCE (S.A.)

1. S.A. = (1/2"/log × No. of logs) + 1/2" (safety factor)
         (12mm/log × No. of logs) + 12mm (safety factor)

2. S.A. = (3/4"/ft. × No. of feet) + 3/4" (safety factor)
         (55mm/meter × No. of meters) + 17mm (safety factor)

The { No. of feet / No. of logs / No. of meters } is simply that "number" of the height within which the builder is concerned about the settling.

CHAPTER 8

Maximum Useage of Logs

This section deals with utilizing material to its fullest extent. One of the most common problems when building is to decide on the maximum length of wall which will accommodate the available material. As a general rule, the proportion of the diameters of the top/butt should be 2/3 or greater. Once the proportion becomes less than 2/3, notching becomes difficult because of the widespread difference in diameters between the butts and the tops. With a large difference in diameters then, a situation will arise where the amount of wood to be removed from the smaller log to fit over a larger one will weaken its structural properties.

The easiest method of overcoming this problem is to have a building design with short enough walls to accommodate the material. In some cases, however, either for structural considerations, design layout, or for personal preference, long walls are required. Three examples on Page 61 show very practical methods of getting the most out of the available material, and still maintaining the optimum dimensional proportions.

Maximum Useage of Logs

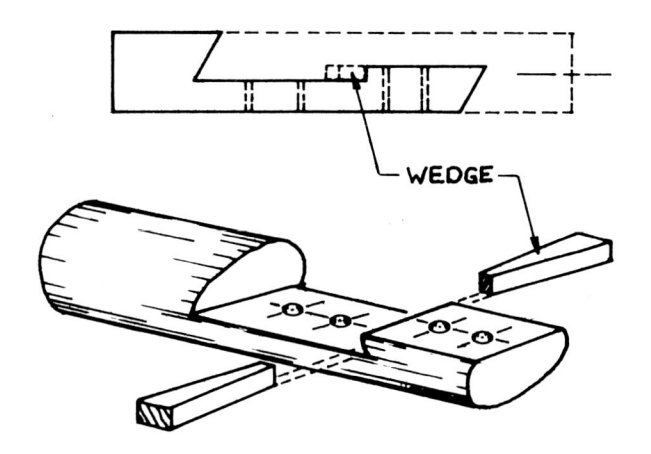

Fig. 13. A splice may be used and the two members, prestressed by wedges, are bolted together. Note that for structural purposes, the bolts are in a horizontal position.

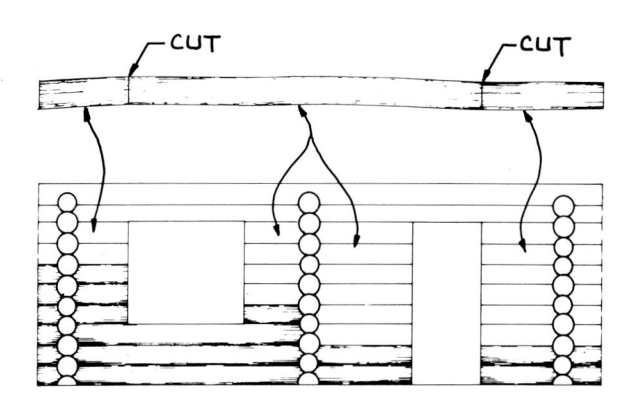

Fig. 14. A rather crooked log may be cut at desired locations and fitted into the building. The window and door locations are of the utmost importance when using this method.

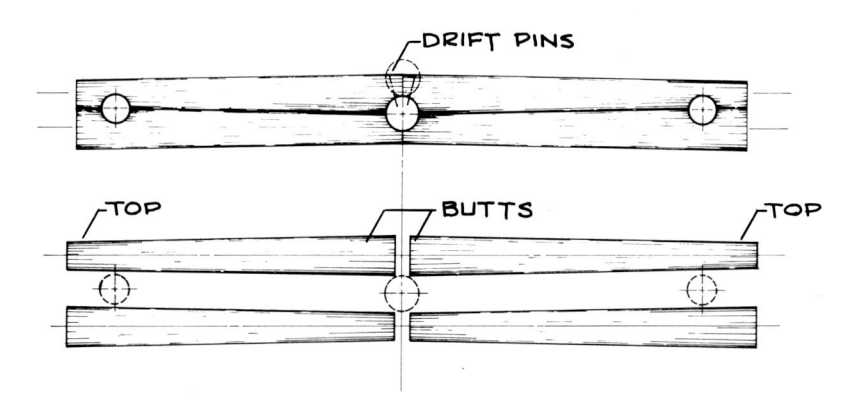

Fig. 15. Joining logs at a notch is also common practice. Since the end of each log is shown with a half-notch, great care must be taken when rolling the log to work on it. At the point where the logs meet, pinning is recommended. Note that when placing the logs on the wall, the butts are mated end-to-end, then on the next round, the tops are mated end-to-end. The reason being that a differential of heights is eliminated where perhaps a butt and top would be mated end-to-end. With this height difference, it becomes increasingly difficult to position the next log to cover the "stepped joint".

The Handbook of Canadian Log Building

Photo 82

CHAPTER 9

Roof Systems

On any building the proportioning of the roof to the walls is critical if a pleasing appearance is to be achieved. Once the walls are erected the next stage is usually the roof support system, which gives the building its ultimate shape and character. A slight change in the inclination of the roof plane will give the structure a totally different view and possibly will provide a different feeling for those who spend a great deal of time in it.

A great deal of time must be spent developing the roof lines to achieve both the aesthetic qualities the builder desires and the functional considerations to which the roof lends itself.

The Handbook of Canadian Log Building

This chapter will deal with some of the most commonly used roof systems, as in Figs. 16-19.

There are, of course, many different styles to choose from and they cannot all be dealt with here, but if the builder studies and understands the layout as well as the functions of all the components of the roof support system in this chapter, this information can then be adapted to develop other roof styles.

Roof Systems

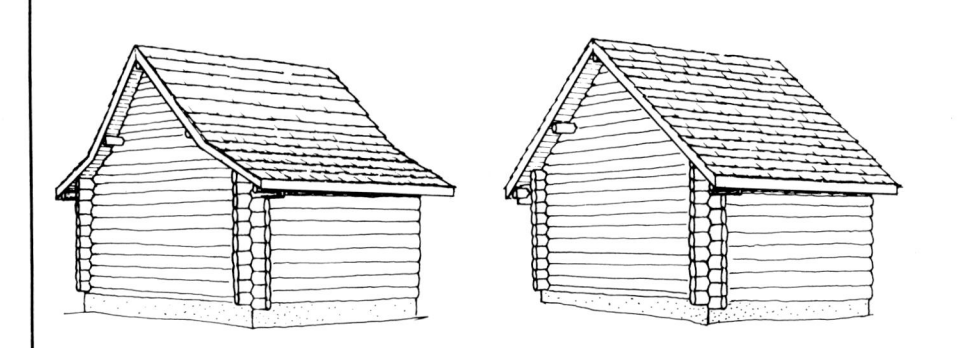

Fig. 16. *The Gable-Roof with an extended overhang. On the left side a change in roof pitch creates a Flare-effect. On the right side the 'outrigger' beam is positioned on the same plane as the main roof.*

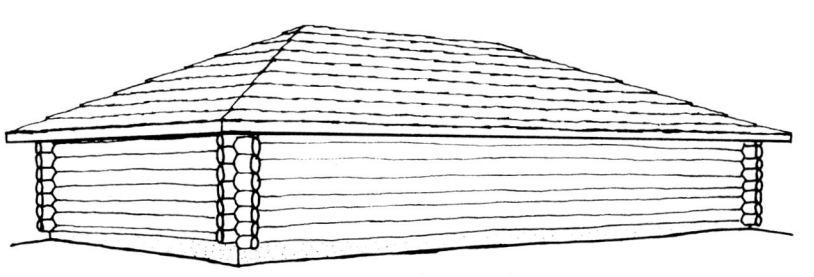

Fig. 17. *The Hip Roof.*

Fig. 18. *The Gable-Roof, using horizontal log gable ends. On the left side a Gable-Dormer is used, and on the right side a Shed-Dormer is used.*

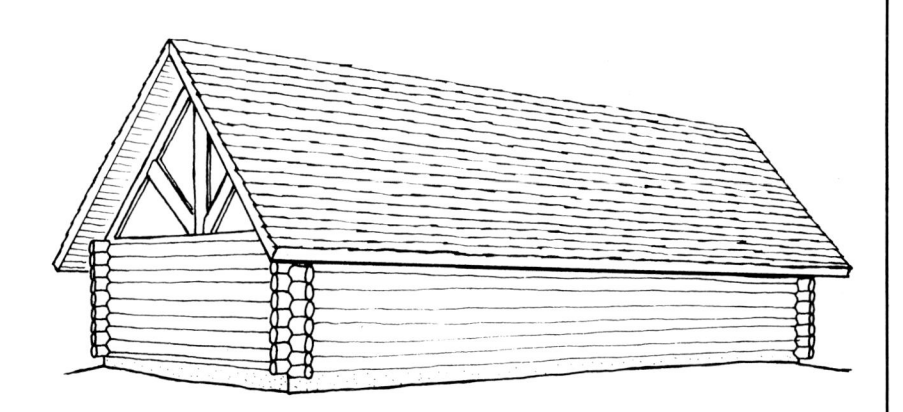

Fig. 19. *The Gable-Roof, using a Trussed-Gable end.*

The Handbook of Canadian Log Building

A variation of the Gable-Roof has unique possibilities brought about by placing "outrigger" beams parallel to the plate log to rest the end of the rafters on. A two-fold design feature has now been accomplished by the addition of these beams. Firstly, a larger and more spacious loft may now be incorporated into what would have normally been a less usable loft area; and secondly, in areas where moisture is a threat to the preservation of the logs, the larger roof overhang now provides for greater diversion of the rains.

In Figs. 20-23, suggestions are made to construct the additional overhang, keeping in mind both the practicality of construction as well as the aesthetics of the building.

Roof Systems

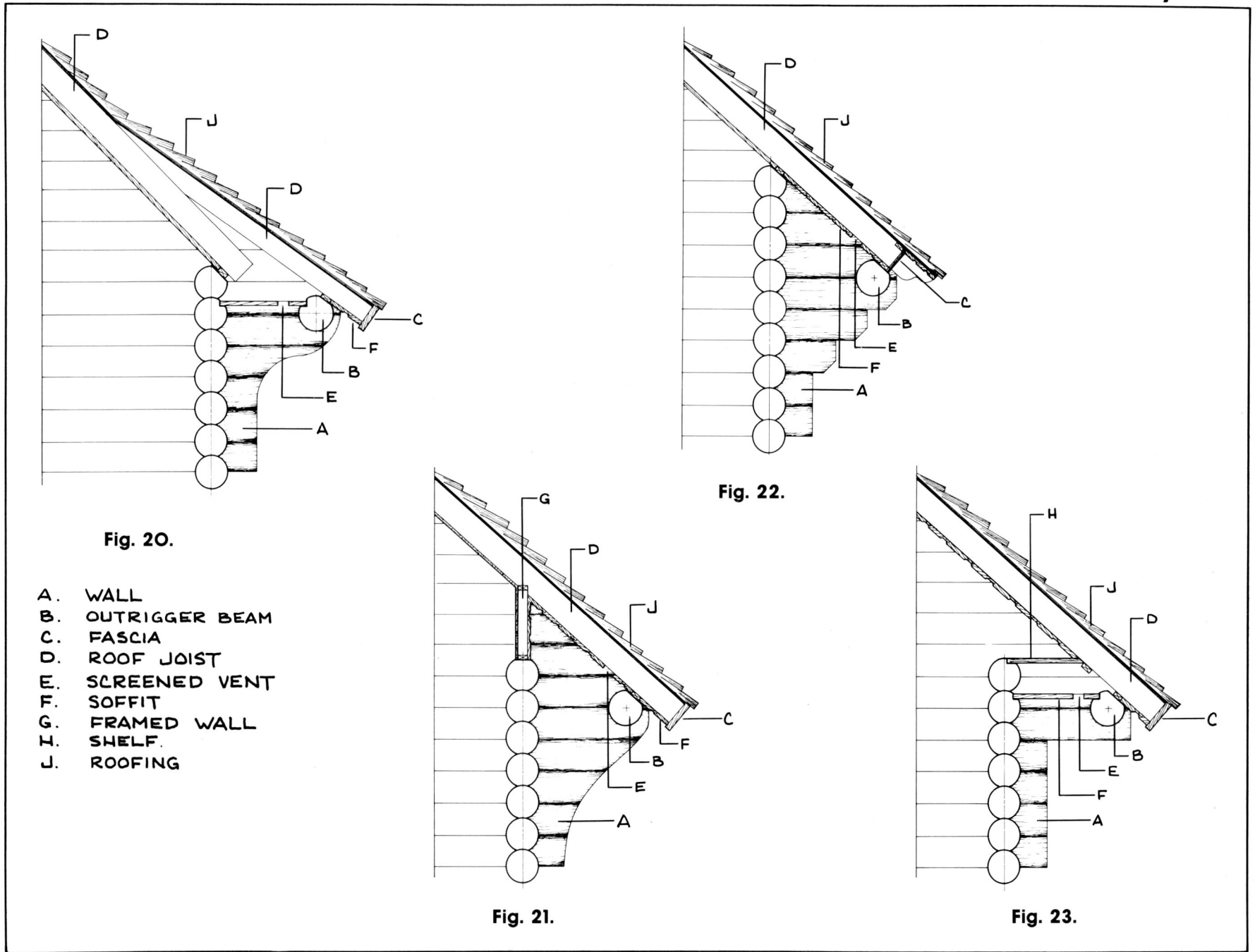

Fig. 20.

Fig. 21.

Fig. 22.

Fig. 23.

A. WALL
B. OUTRIGGER BEAM
C. FASCIA
D. ROOF JOIST
E. SCREENED VENT
F. SOFFIT
G. FRAMED WALL
H. SHELF
J. ROOFING

67

The Handbook of Canadian Log Building

If horizontal log gable ends are used, then settling of the logs which make up the gable becomes a major factor. Because the distance or height between the peak of the roof and the plate log is constantly diminishing, then the roofing must be constructed to allow for this continually changing dimension. Two methods for consideration are as follows:

Fig. 24 illustrates that the gable logs are in fact 'sandwiched' between rafters and the decking is applied to the underside of the roof joists. Fig. 25 illustrates that the gable end is grooved to allow a spline and insulation to be inserted in the log gable, and the spline then attached to the decking. This provides for an airtight seal and at the same time, stabilizes the gable end. Once again, the decking is shown on the underside of the roof joist. Should the builder decide to place the decking on the top side of the roof joist, care must be taken in selecting the roof joists because they will be, in fact, exposed.

The roof framing above the decking follows standard building practices and must comply with local regulations. Note on the illustrations that the roof joists are attached firmly to the ridge-pole. Metal guide bars are attached at the plate log, and the roof joists are then bolted in such a way as to allow DOWNWARD movement as the gable settles. At the purlins wooden guide blocks may be adequate, depending of course on spacing and roof load.

Roof Systems

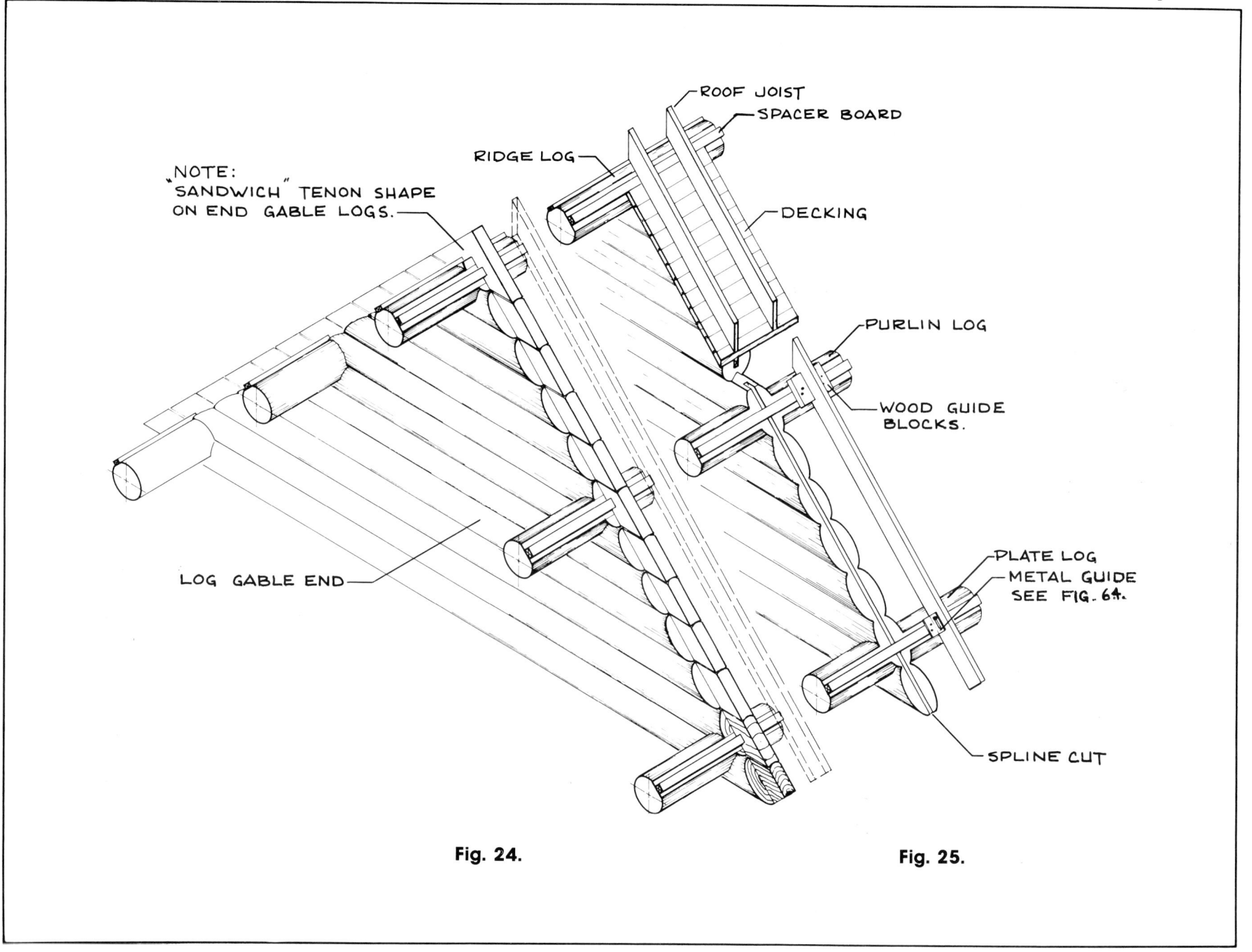

Fig. 24.

Fig. 25.

69

The Handbook of Canadian Log Building

It is essential with roof work to establish a starting point for the layout. Since logs aren't uniform in nature the heights of the various corners of the building will differ. As well, the distance between centrelines of the walls will vary, although this should be minimal. The builder who is keen and methodical about the layout procedures and material selection will understand that as the last few rounds are being built, careful log selection will prove invaluable when the final layout stage is reached. In other words, keep the difference in heights and widths to a minimum. An experienced builder will understand that control of heights through selection of the correct-sized material is better than altering the optimum scribing distance to achieve correct wall height.

The first step in the layout is to choose a common height or PLATE LINE based on the lowest corner of the building and a common WIDTH, which is based on the narrowest end of the building. Once a horizontal and level plane has been established to work to, and a predetermined width has been achieved, the triangular shape must be completed by establishing a height. In short, consider a common builder's term – SLOPE. SLOPE is a term used to indicate the angle at which the roof is designed. Rather than an angular term, the SLOPE is defined as "rise divided by run". An example of the terms used to this point is illustrated in Fig. 26.

Roof Systems

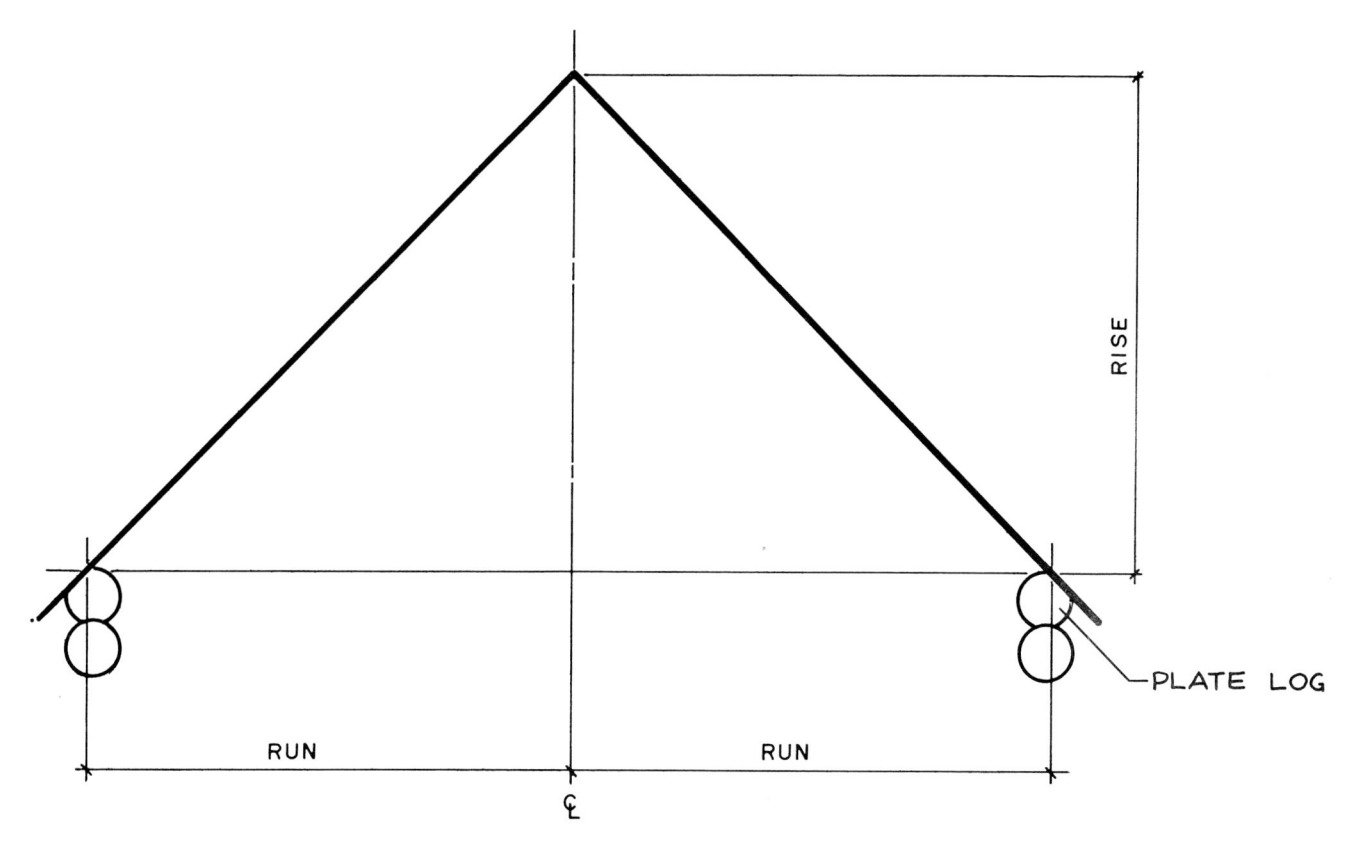

Fig. 26. Basic Layout Procedure

Through the use of geometry, calculations may be done to determine the angle, but it is the intention of this text to simplify roof construction as much as possible by eliminating unnecessary calculations.

The Handbook of Canadian Log Building

In essence, what has been accomplished to this point is to design a triangle *within* which the main roof frame will be constructed.

At this point there are several choices the builder must consider as to exactly what may be built within the 'triangle'. First consider what is called a "single-framed roof" and then a "double-framed roof". Quite simply, a "single-framed roof" would consist of a series of trusses in a row, with the roof sheathing applied directly to them. This is a very common method of roofing used in conventional framing. Fig. 27, illustrates the most common types of trusses.

A "double-framed roof" is simply fewer trusses engineered for greater spacing, and horizontal beams (roof beams) placed above them; then the roof is constructed on top of the roof beams as illustrated in Fig. 28.

Once some sort of design consideration has been established, it becomes the responsibility of the designer to properly select the truss configuration as well as the spacing of the trusses for the building, depending on structural and aesthetic qualities.

Roof Systems

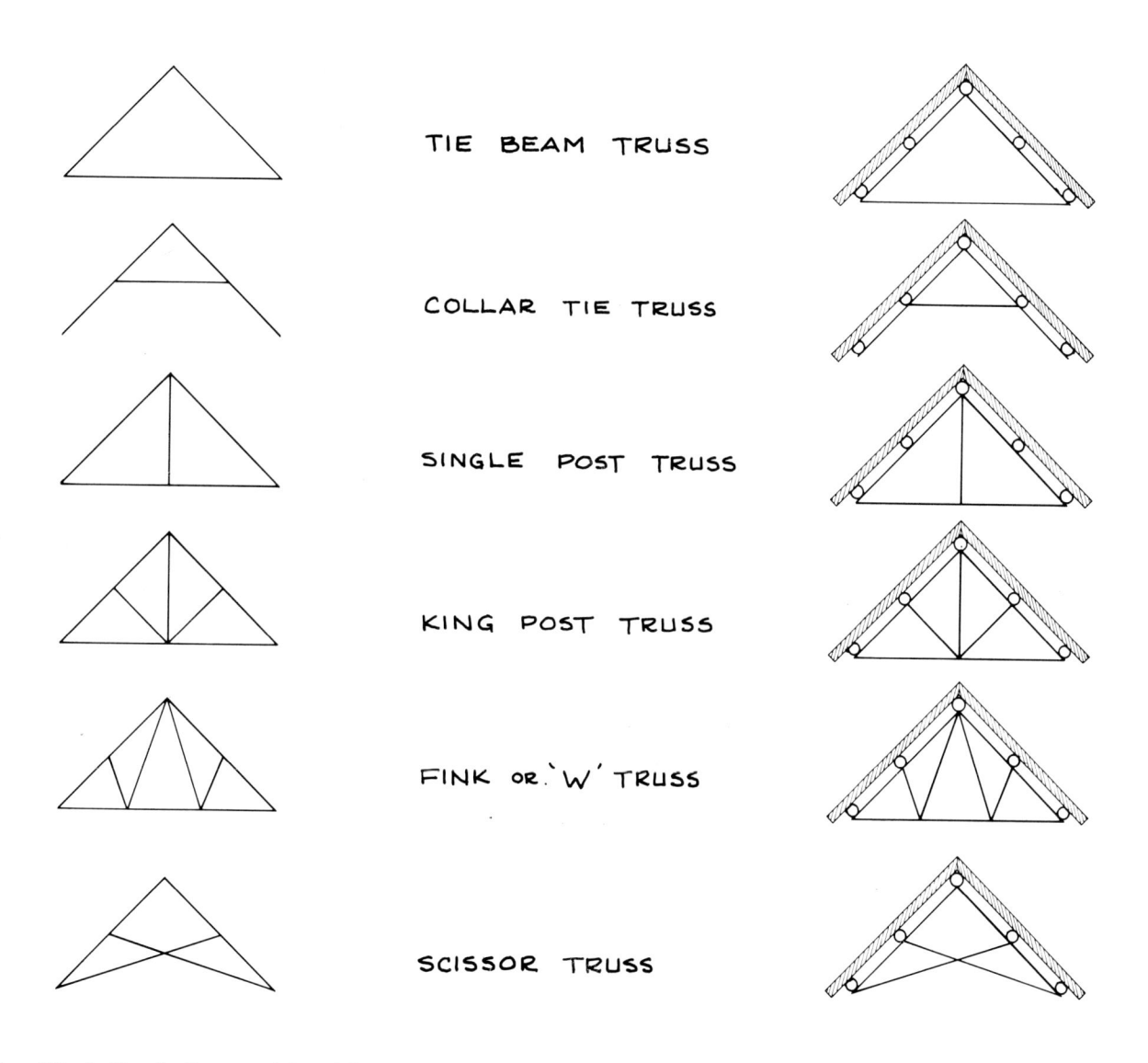

TIE BEAM TRUSS

COLLAR TIE TRUSS

SINGLE POST TRUSS

KING POST TRUSS

FINK OR 'W' TRUSS

SCISSOR TRUSS

Fig. 27. *A Single-Framed Roof System.*

Fig. 28. *A Double-framed Roof System.*

The Handbook of Canadian Log Building

Should the builder wish to use other materials or combinations of materials to construct the gable ends for contrast or aesthetic qualities, then this section will be of great importance.

Now it's time to consider the components of a basic roof support system. Generally the ridge-pole is flattened on two sides at the same angle as the roof to accept ease in framing of the roof. In addition, there should be flattened seats at the beaming locations, the trusses and/or gables. If any sort of framework is incorporated into the log truss or gable, then it's recommended that the components of either the truss or gable be flattened for ease of framing. See Fig. 29.

Note also that the purlins and platelogs are flattened on the top sides for ease of installing the roof joists. A "spacer" board, the thickness of the ceiling material, is nailed along the surface of all the roof beams. When the time comes to install the ceiling material, it may be inserted between the roof beams and the roof joists, thus eliminating the need to scribe the ceiling material to the irregular surface of the roof beams.

In Fig. 30, notice that the members of the truss are flattened and a splined joint is used. In Fig. 31, the dimensional lumber is nailed and glued to the truss members.

Roof Systems

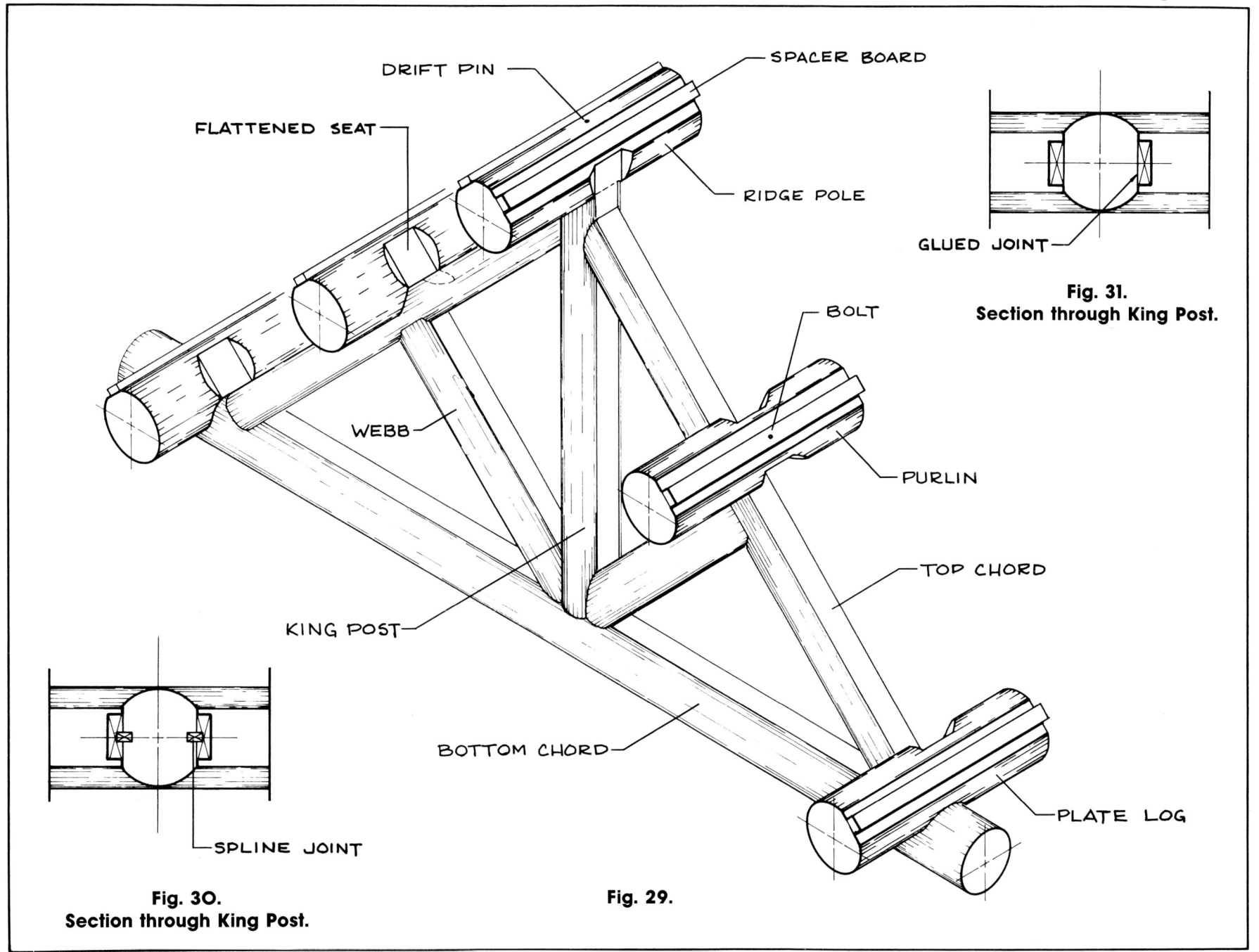

Fig. 31.
Section through King Post.

Fig. 30.
Section through King Post.

Fig. 29.

75

The Handbook of Canadian Log Building

If, however, no such framing is required, then only the top side of the top chord need be flattened for the purlins, as in Fig. 32.

We must now examine the different possibilities of joinery for the various truss components.

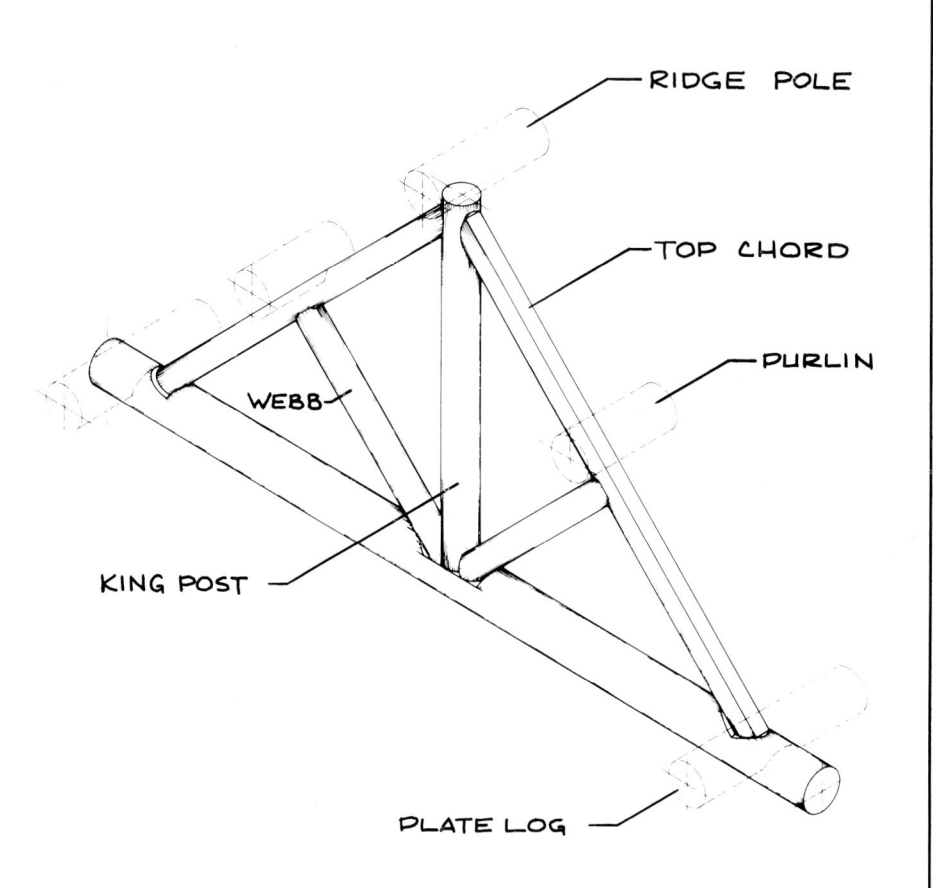

Fig. 32.

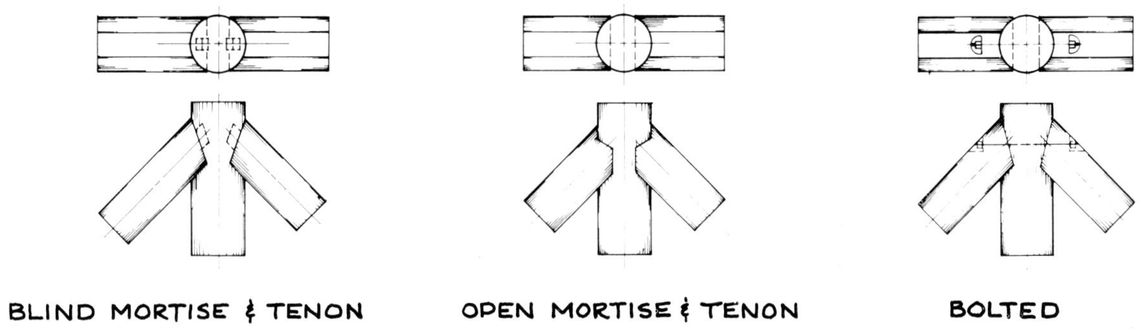

Roof Systems

BLIND MORTISE & TENON OPEN MORTISE & TENON BOLTED

DRIFT PIN

DETAIL A: *Various types of joinery at the junction of the* top-chords *and the* king-post.

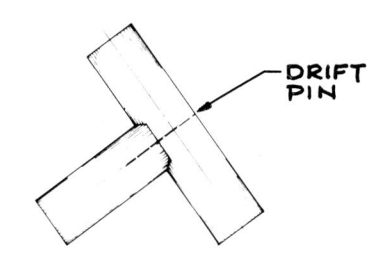

DETAIL B: *Typical joint at the junction of the* top-chord *and the* webb.

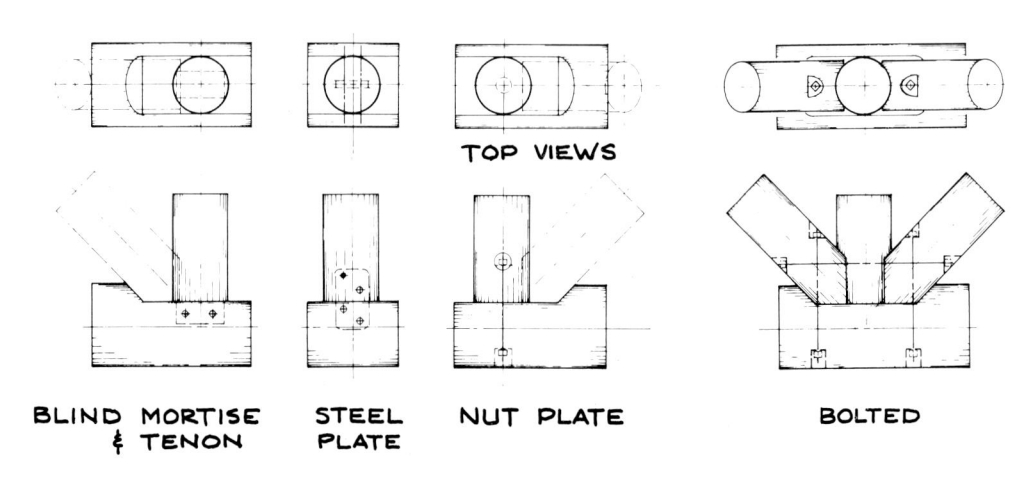

TOP VIEWS

BLIND MORTISE & TENON   STEEL PLATE   NUT PLATE   BOLTED

END VIEW

BOLTED   BLIND MORTISE & TENON

DETAIL C: *Various types of joinery at the junction of the* king-post *and the* bottom-chord.

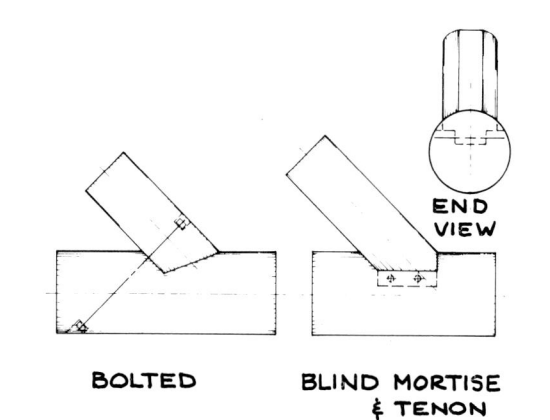

DETAIL D: *Typical joints at the junction of the* top-chord *and the* bottom-chord.

The Handbook of Canadian Log Building

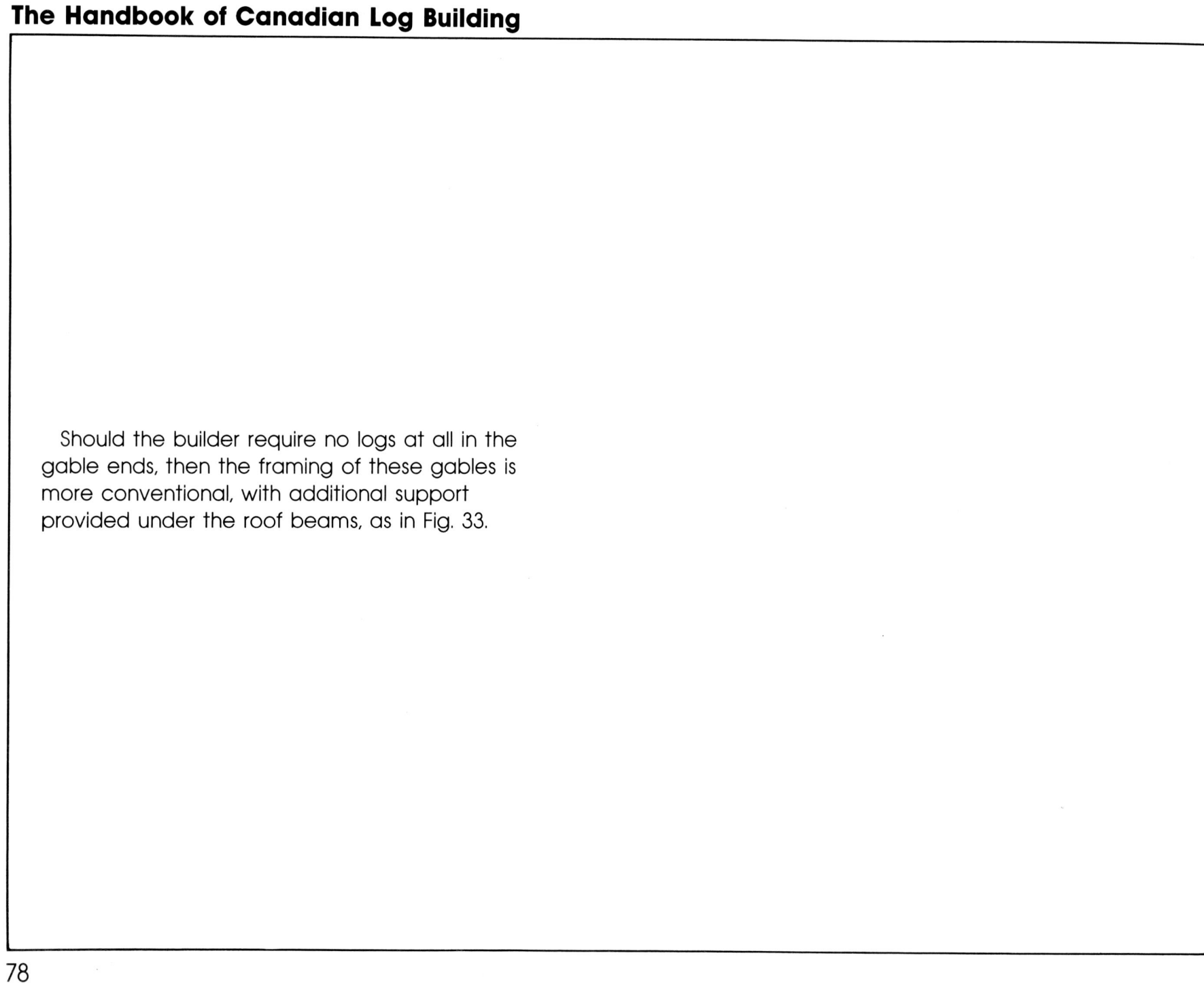

Should the builder require no logs at all in the gable ends, then the framing of these gables is more conventional, with additional support provided under the roof beams, as in Fig. 33.

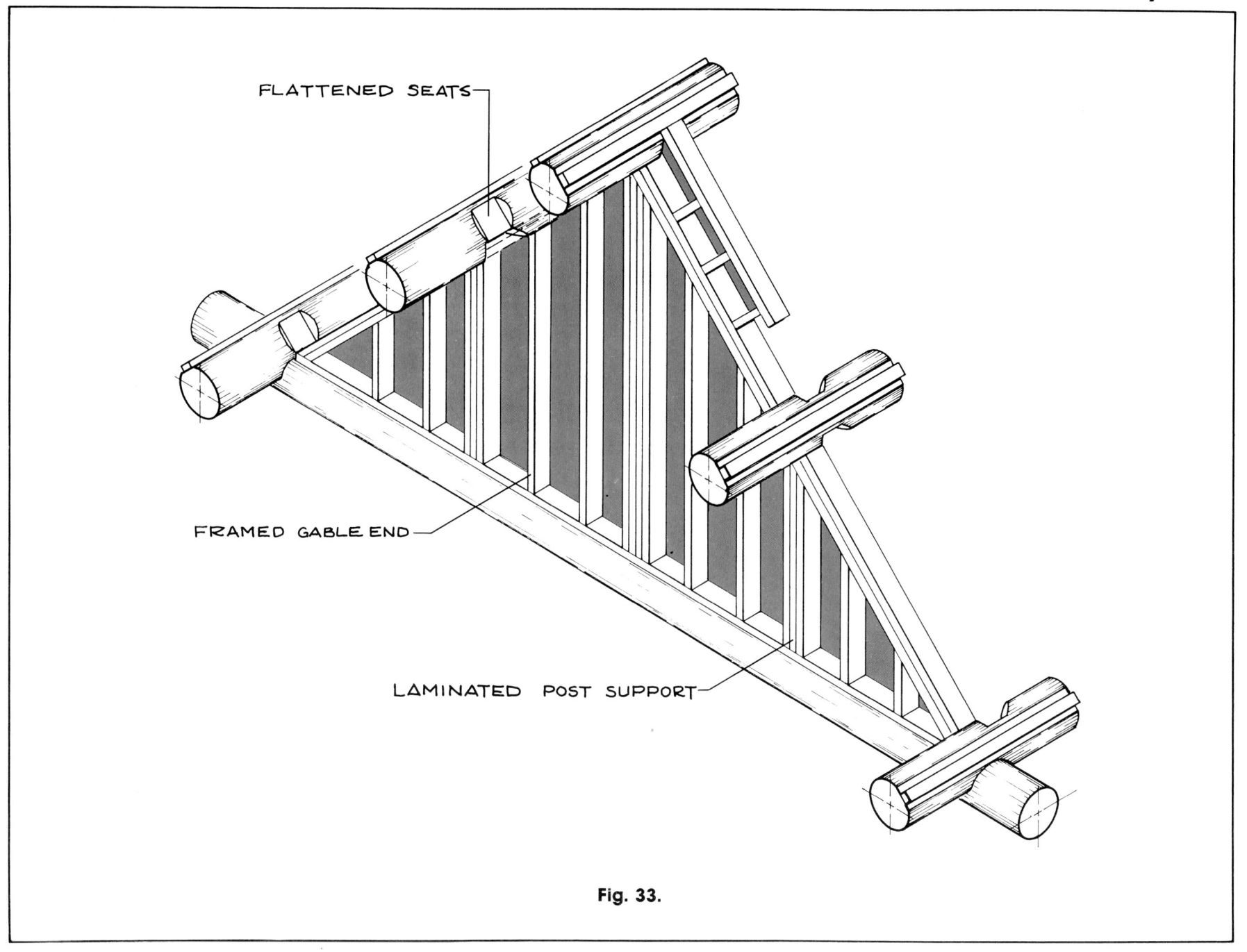

Roof Systems

FLATTENED SEATS

FRAMED GABLE END

LAMINATED POST SUPPORT

Fig. 33.

The Handbook of Canadian Log Building

Once the builder has digested all the possible combinations of roof support systems and types of joinery, it becomes a matter of choosing the best possible combinations to fit the circumstances and then constructing the roof system accordingly. What the builder must do now is simply build the gables and/or trusses *within* the triangular dimensions which have been laid out by determining the common plate line and the common width line.

The key point to remember is that the sloping lines in the calculations represent the *bottom* of the roof joists, and therefore the plate logs must be flattened over their full length to allow for easy framing of the roof.

Roof Systems

Photo 83 A

Photo 83 B

Photo 83 C

Photo 83 D

Photo 83 E

Photo 83 F

Photo 83 G

Photo 83 H

Photo 83 I

81

The Handbook of Canadian Log Building

In areas where long, continuous timbers of uniform diameters are plentiful, a roof system like that shown in Fig. 34 should be considered. If, however, the builder is confronted with a situation where a long, continuous roof line is required but the material is not suitable. then an alternate system as shown in Fig. 35 could be considered, using one of the two possible types of joinery at the purlin/top chord intersection. In Fig. 36, a view of the purlin with the tenon-joint is shown, along with a view of the purlin with a half-lapped dovetail-joint. Extra layout and notching is required for this system, but if it's done carefully and accurately, it may lend itself to a great variety of conditions.

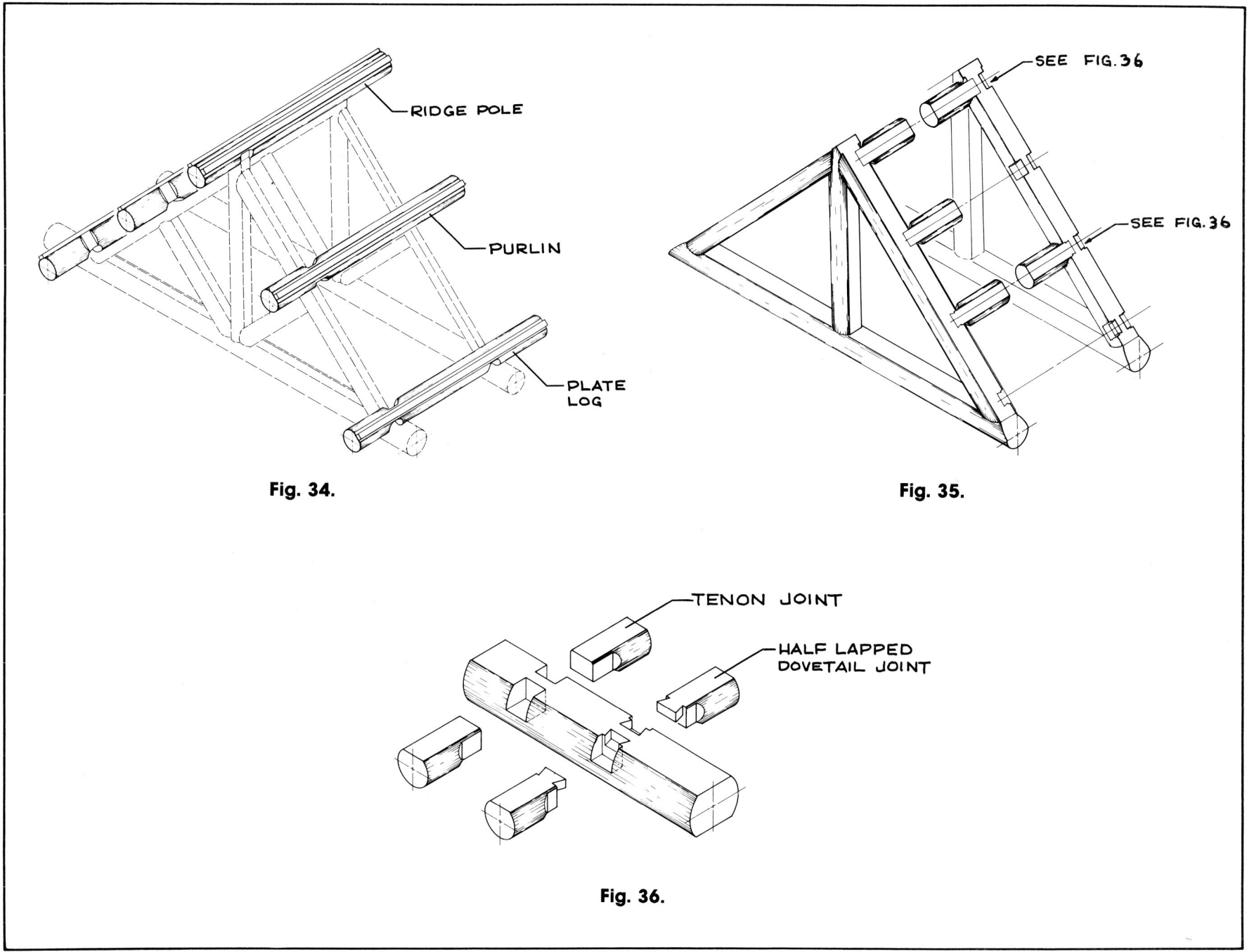

Roof Systems

Fig. 34.

Fig. 35.

Fig. 36.

The Handbook of Canadian Log Building

Photo 84 A

Photo 84 C

Photo 84 B

84

CHAPTER 10

Window and Door Installation

Windows and doors are installed by very similar methods, with the only difference being that, unlike windows, in most cases door openings are cut with no sills. The builder does, however, have the option of cutting a door sill if one is desired.

First the builder must know the exact location of the door or window opening to be cut. This is usually achieved by locating a centre-line on the surface of the log wall. From this line, measurements are taken to the left and right. The total width of the opening will be the sum of all the components of the opening:

(1) the width of the window or door, including its frame,
(2) the shim space on both sides of the window or door,
(3) the thickness of the wooden nailer to which the window or door frame will be attached.

The total height of the opening to be cut will again be the total of all its components:

(1) the height of the window or door, including its frame,

The Handbook of Canadian Log Building

(2) the shim space at the bottom of the window or door,

(3) the settling space allowed at the top of the window or door (using the FORMULAS in Chapter 7).

Actual calculations for the cut lines are shown written on the logs (to be erased after the cuts are made) on page 88 (Figs. 40 and 41.)

Usually a level line is placed on the logs to mark the location of the top and bottom cuts, and particular attention is given to NOT cutting more than one-half of either the top log or the bottom log to accommodate the window or door. See Fig. 37 &

Photo 85

Fig. 37

Photo 86

Fig. 38

Window and Door Installation

Fig. 38. Pieces of "straight" dimensional lumber are used as guides for making the two vertical cuts, as in Fig. 40 & Fig. 41. Care must be taken when making these cuts, because errors in cutting will result in either a great deal of touch-up work, or enlarging the opening to accommodate larger windows or doors.

To make the top and bottom cuts horizontal, the builder should use whatever scaffolding is available to work in a comfortable position. It is recommended that all horizontal cuts be made by cutting to a depth of no more than 2 inches 5 cm) along the entire line of cut. Then return to the original starting point and make another cut, with its depth no more than 2 inches (5 cm). Repeat this procedure until the full penetration of the wall is complete. See Fig. 39.

Photo 87

Fig. 39.

87

The Handbook of Canadian Log Building

To make the two (vertical) side cuts, a two-step procedure should be followed. First, nail a piece of dimensional lumber (plumb) alongside the mark placed on the wall; that will be the cut line. Then, assuming a comfortable stance, position your body so your shoulders are parallel to an imaginary line through the centre of the length of the log wall. Now, by concentrating on a perfect plumb cut, merely make a cut approximately one inch (2.5 cm) deep along the intended line of cut. See Fig. 40.

Next, remove the guide boards and again, positioned as with the initial cut, penetrate through the wall for the final cut. See Fig. 41. Full control of the chainsaw is necessary to eliminate the possibility of overcutting any of the cuts in the corners of the opening. Any error at this point will result in an unsatisfactory job.

Photo 88

Photo 89

Fig. 40.

Fig. 41.

Window and Door Installation

After the main opening is cut in the wall, it becomes necessary to adequately stabilize the structure, while still allowing the logwork to settle around the window or door. The method used, is to install a spline (in a PLUMB position) to which the window (or door) nailer is attached. As the builder will notice in Fig. 46, the spline and the 'nailer' are actually a combined unit to lessen air infiltration at this location.

Photo 90

Photo 91

Photo 92

Fig. 42

Fig. 43

Fig. 44

89

The Handbook of Canadian Log Building

As in Figs. 42-43, a series of chainsaw cuts are made to remove enough wood to allow the spline to be freely installed. It is most important here that the spline move easily into the cavity, to allow for the unobstructed movement of the logs.

Once all the chainsaw cuts have been made, as seen in Fig. 44, all cut surfaces should be dressed smoothly by either sanding (Fig. 45) or planing, and all sharp edges removed. Then all the components are installed (Fig. 47) and the window (or door) insulated and trimmed to its finished appearance. The trim board on top is allowed to slide freely down past the window frame. The builder should realize that this upper settling space need not remain unfinished, but may actually be trimmed in a pleasing and practical manner.

Photo 93

Fig. 45.

Window and Door Installation

Photo 94

Photo 95

Fig. 46.

Fig. 47

91

The Handbook of Canadian Log Building

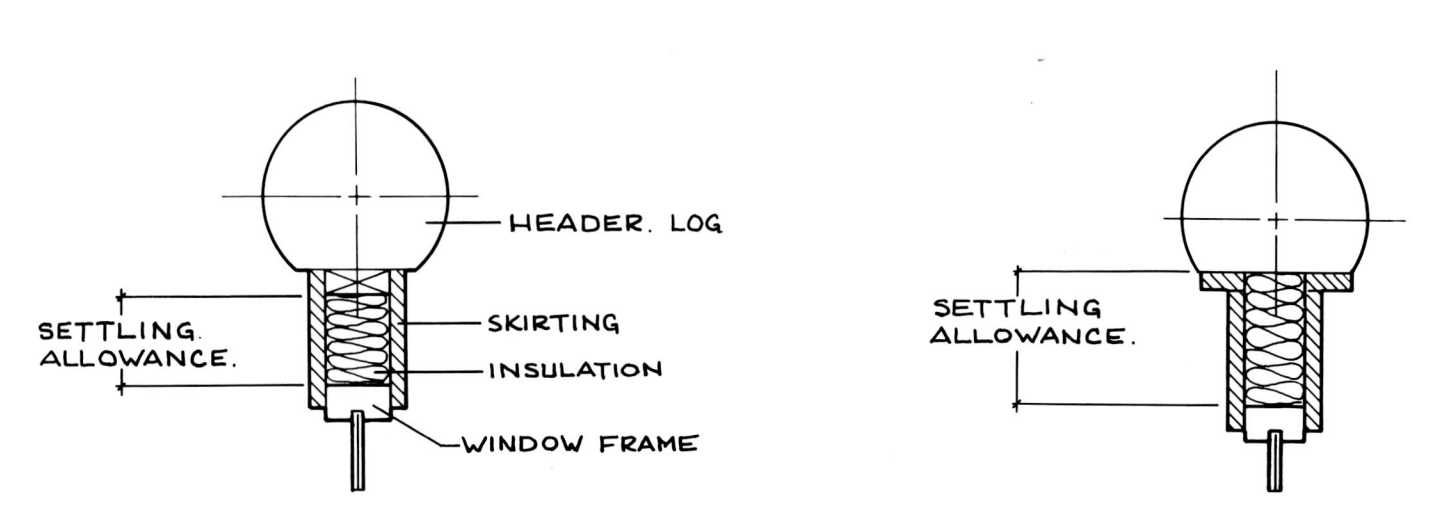

Fig. 48. *Side View, with the skirting attached by an internal fastener.*

Fig. 49. *Side View, with the skirting attached by an external fastener.*

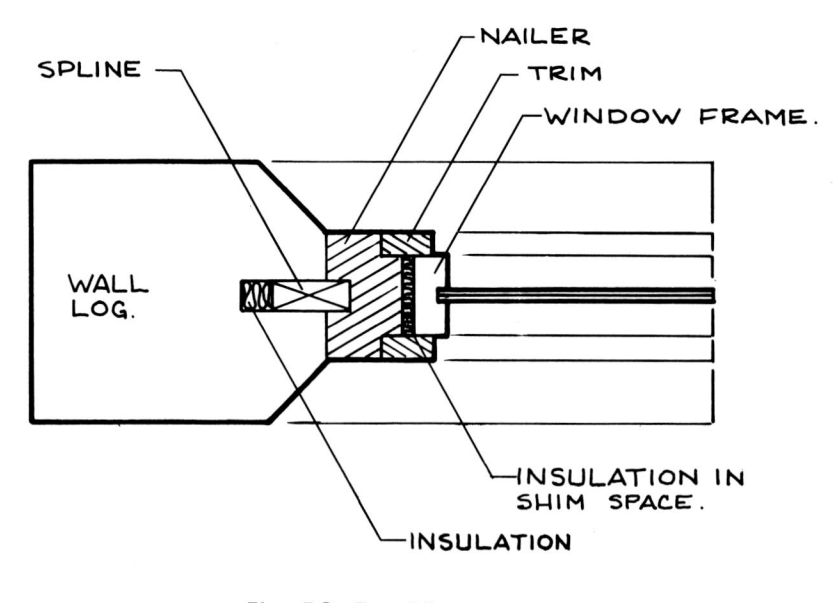

Fig. 50. *Top View.*

Window and Door Installation

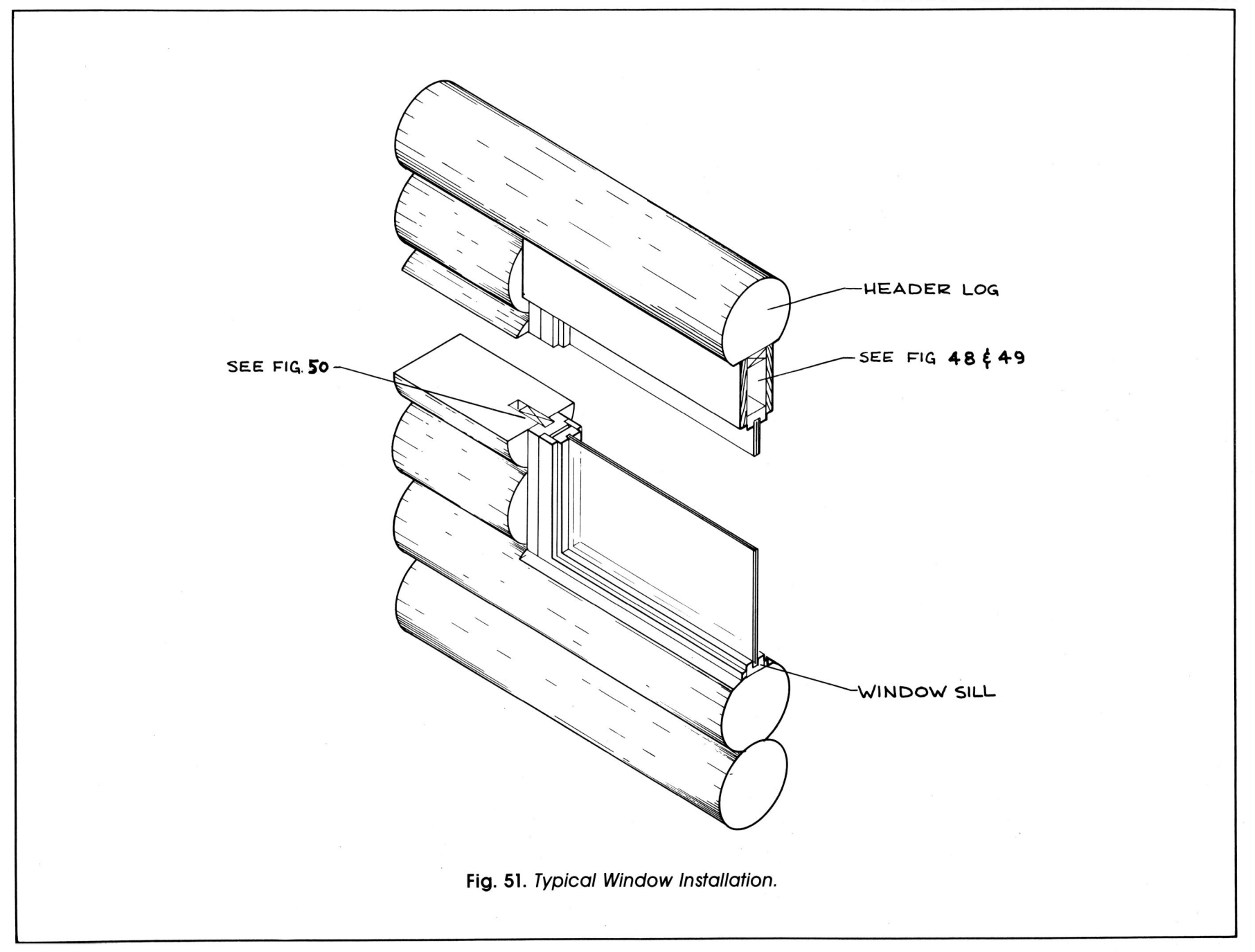

Fig. 51. *Typical Window Installation.*

The Handbook of Canadian Log Building

Photo 96

Photo 97

94

CHAPTER 11

Partitions

The following techniques deal with attaching framed walls to log walls, but prior to beginning this phase the builder should understand that if renovations are done later, a permanent and perhaps unsightly scar will remain on the wall. In addition, it must be remembered that the installation of framed partitions has unique considerations brought about by the settling conditions common to log structures.

The first rule of 'partitioning' is to locate the precise position where the partition is to fit into a log wall and then work from a centre line at this point, calculating the exact thickness of that partition wall (the framing width along with the thickness of the materials applied to each side of the partition). Do this for each partition at each wall. When the total thickness of the partition is known, allow a slight margin to ensure ease when inserting the partition into the cut in the log wall. Then make the final marks on the wall for cutting.

There are several methods of cutting the log wall to accept framing, but to avoid confusing the issue only one will be discussed here. Simply attach to the log wall (in a perfectly PLUMB position), two pieces of dimensional lumber spaced at the

The Handbook of Canadian Log Building

required thickness of the framed wall. Using these as guides, saw cuts can then be made into the log walls to accept the frame work. Note that, when cutting the channel in the wall to accept the framed partitions, care must be taken not to cut too deeply and so weaken the log wall.

It must be noted here that the height of the partition wall must be less than the height of the beams or ceiling materials above that wall, to allow for settling. The required difference in height may be calculated using the settling formula in Chapter 7. For the final appearance a trim board is attached to the ceiling materials in such a way that it may slide freely down past the side of the partition framing.

It is most important that the builder realizes this upper settling space need not remain unfinished; it may be trimmed in a very pleasing and practical manner.

Prior to inserting the framework, be sure to smooth the exposed cut edges of the logs, using a chisel, a sander or a plane. Then, as noted in Fig. 54, the framed wall stud attached to the log wall must be fixed in such a fashion as to allow for the constant movement and settling of the logs. One good building technique is to cut about three vertical slots in the stud and then, using either large nails or lag blots, connect the framed wall to the log wall by placing the nails or bolts at or near the TOP of the slots. See Fig. 54. Again, the required length for each slot may be calculated using the settling formula in Chapter 7.

Partitions

Photo 98

Photo 99

Photo 100

The Handbook of Canadian Log Building

Care must be taken when installing the partition but remember that framed walls installed with good taste can provide a nice contrast which will ultimately enhance the beauty of carefully-fitted log work.

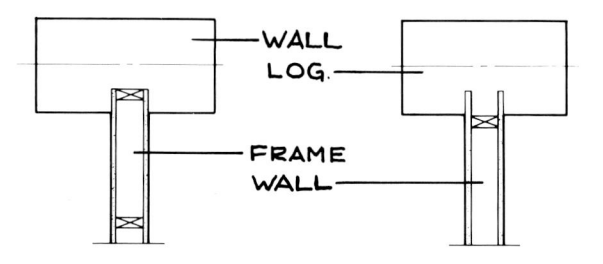

Fig. 52. *On left: the framed wall stud is cut into the logwork. On right: the partitioning material only is cut into the logwork.*

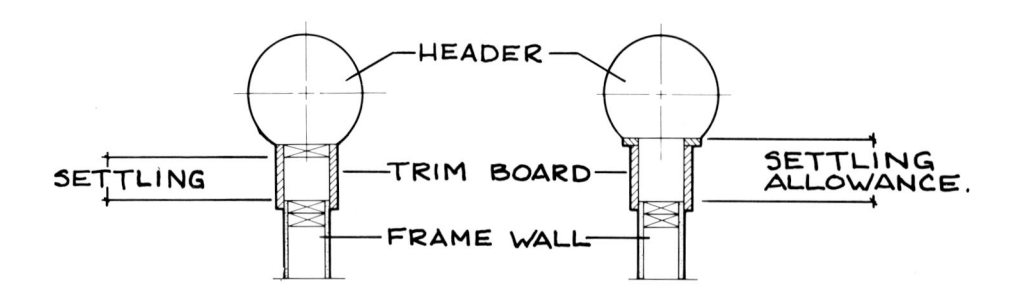

Fig. 53. *On left: the trim board is attached to the overhead beam by an internal fastener. On right: the trim board is attached to the overhead beam by an external fastener.*

Partitions

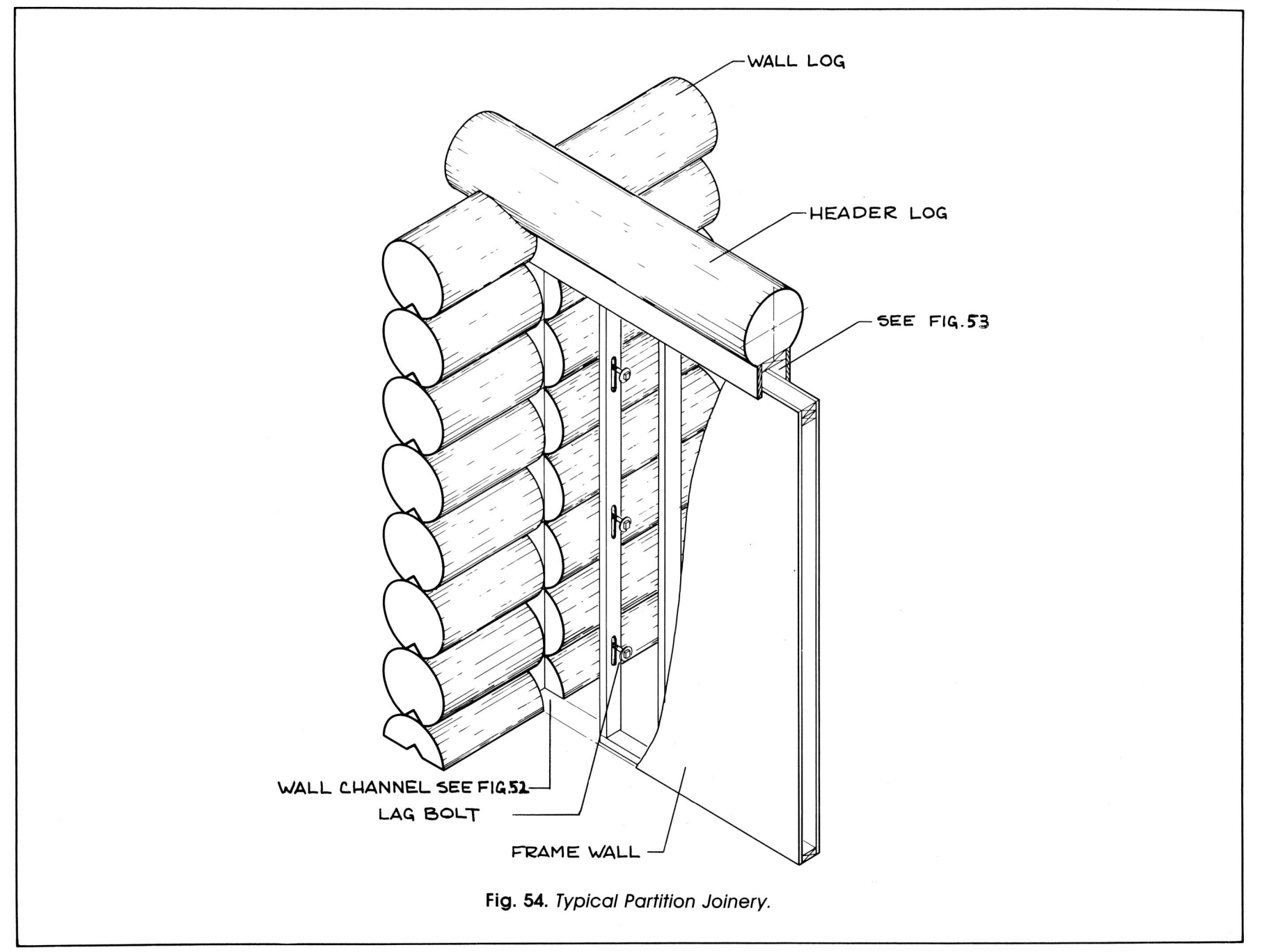

Fig. 54. *Typical Partition Joinery.*

The Handbook of Canadian Log Building

Photo 101

Photo 102

CHAPTER 12

Cabinet Installation

Once again due to the effects of settling, cabinet installation requires much forethought. Cabinets cannot be attached directly to the log walls, but must be attached in such a way that the logs may settle without interfering with the cabinet's components.

There are basically two methods of incorporating cabinets into the logwork of a building. The first, as in Fig. 55, is to build a framed wall inside the log wall and then attach the cabinets to the framed wall only. The framed wall is attached to the log wall in a similar fashion to that used with partition walls as discussed in Chapter 11.

The second method, as in Fig. 58, involves building the cabinets in such a way that the cabinet's gables are wider than the cabinets themselves. A cut is then made in the log wall to accept the gable, and the cabinets may be set in place and anchored to a sliding nailer. The slot in the wall makes for a neat, finished appearance, and also enables ease in cleaning.

The Handbook of Canadian Log Building

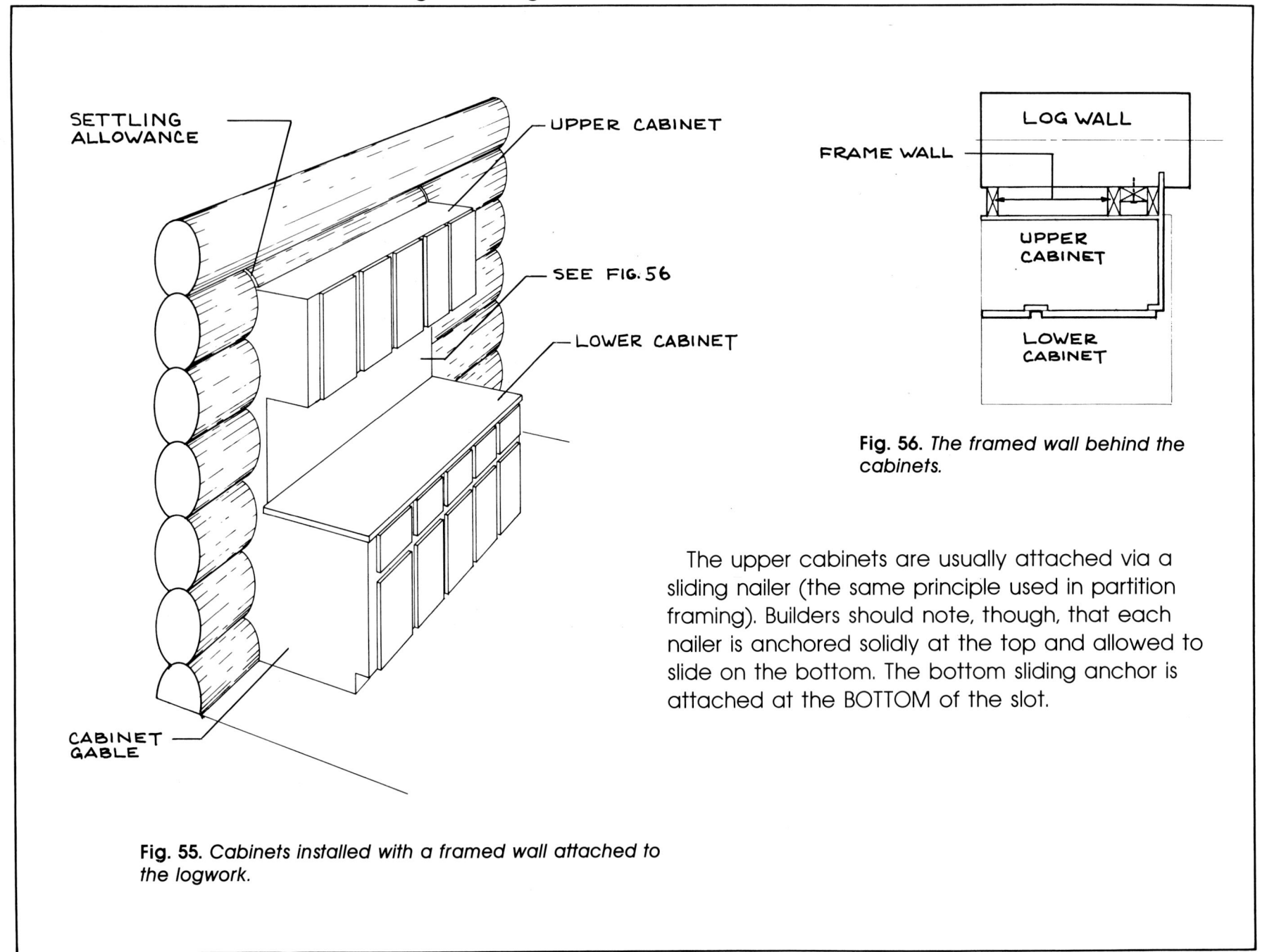

Fig. 56. *The framed wall behind the cabinets.*

The upper cabinets are usually attached via a sliding nailer (the same principle used in partition framing). Builders should note, though, that each nailer is anchored solidly at the top and allowed to slide on the bottom. The bottom sliding anchor is attached at the BOTTOM of the slot.

Fig. 55. *Cabinets installed with a framed wall attached to the logwork.*

Cabinet Installation

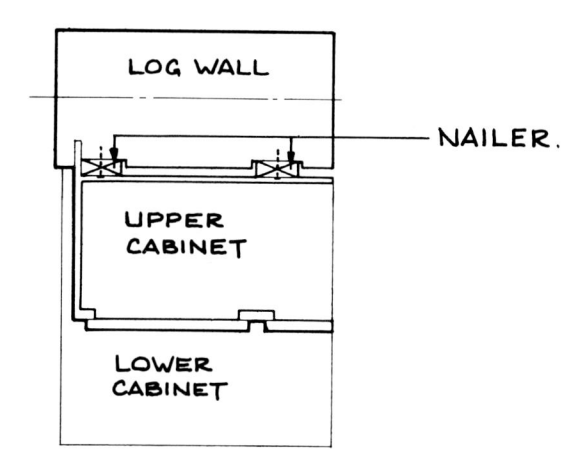

Fig. 57. *The sliding nailer behind the cabinets.*

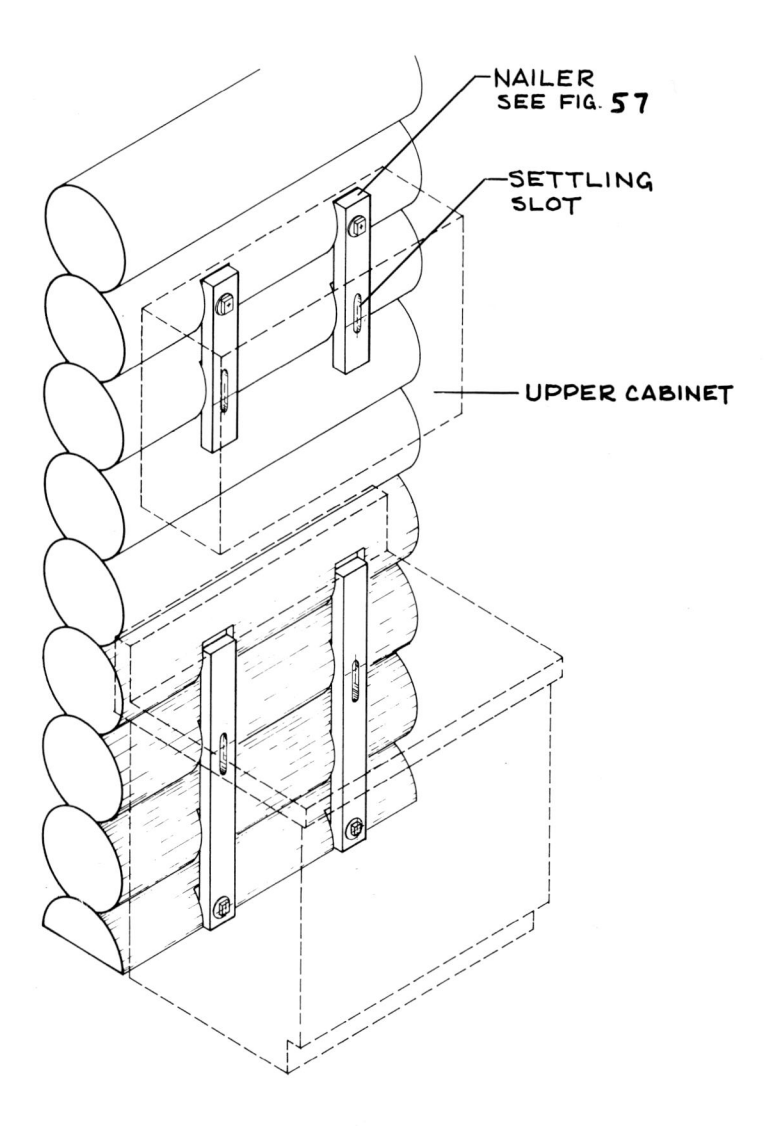

Fig. 58. *Cabinets installed with a sliding nailer.*

103

The Handbook of Canadian Log Building

Photo 103

CHAPTER 13

Chimneys

Again due to the ever-present factor of the settling process which affects log structures, the chimney must be built in such a way that the roof can settle down around it.

Flashing is attached to the roof in a conventional manner, and then a counter-flashing is used to provide for a weatherproof seal while at the same time allowing for the inevitable settling. See Figs. 59 and 60.

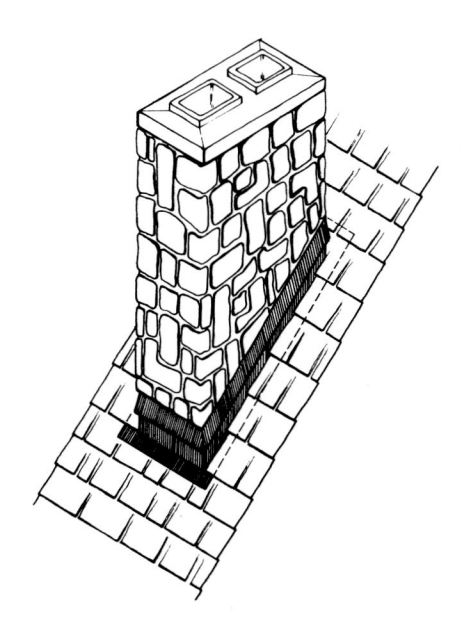

Fig. 59.

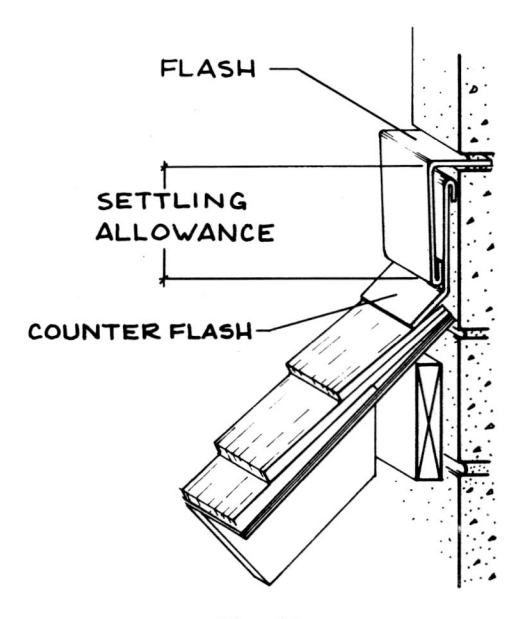

Fig. 60.

The Handbook of Canadian Log Building

Photo 104

Good planning will ensure that the chimney is strategically located, so it will fit between ceiling beams and alongside trusses, so none of these will have to be cut and thus ruin the structural capabilities for which they were designed.

Photo 105

106

CHAPTER 14

Electrical Installation

An essential aspect of planning a log building is a complete and comprehensive electrical layout. Builders should keep in mind that it is advisable to place all wires vertically whenever possible, not in the lateral grooves between the logs.

In most cases, the wiring for a log building may be planned to fit into one of four categories, as in Fig. 61.

A) Partition wiring is recommended wherever possible which allows for easy access when drilling the framework,

B) Switch outlets which are usually located beside doorways, and the wiring concealed behind the keyway of the door opening. It is normal building practice to cut the keyway deeper than that required for merely the spline, to allow for ease in wiring. The overhead lighting may then be

The Handbook of Canadian Log Building

wired above the doorway and into the ceiling or roof framing system,

C) Kitchen cabinet receptacles may be wired behind the cabinets, with no drilling in the logwork, and the boxes installed in the splashback above the countertop,

D) Electrical wiring for the base plugs. Usually these plugs are located within 18 inches (46 cm) of the floor. It should be noted that the electrical outlets may be installed in either the first or second round of logs.

In cases A, B and C, very little explanation is required because all fit into near standard electrical procedures. However, in case D, a recommended procedure to facilitate the installation of the boxes is as follows:

FIRST AND FOREMOST, AFTER THE SECOND ROUND OF LOGS HAVE BEEN FITTED DURING THE CONSTRUCTION PROCESS, THE LAYOUT FOR ALL THE BASE-PLUGS MUST BE COMPLETED, COMPLYING TO LOCAL BUILDING REQUIREMENTS.

Electrical Installation

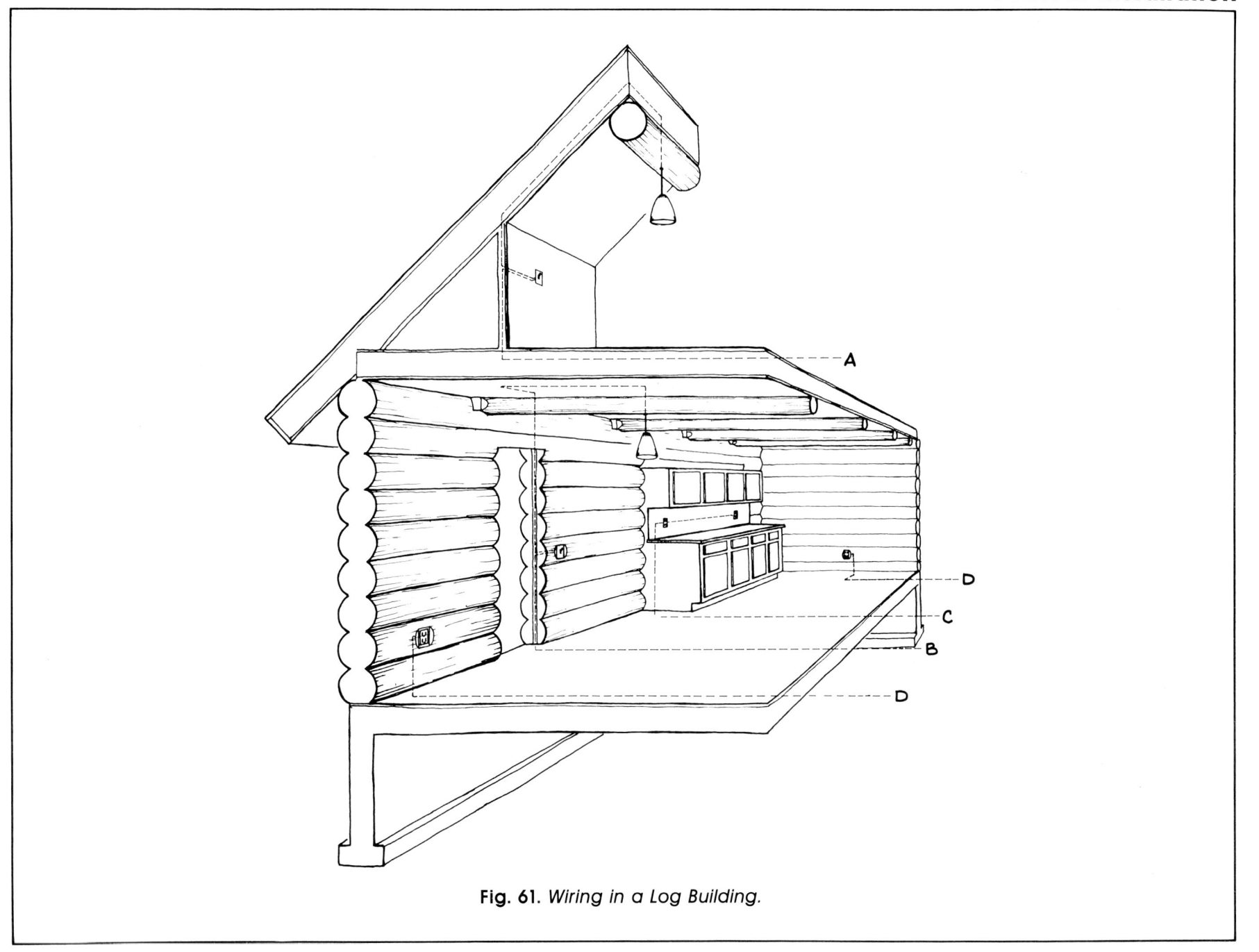

Fig. 61. *Wiring in a Log Building.*

109

The Handbook of Canadian Log Building

Photo 106

STEP 1: *At the location of each outlet, carefully mark the outline of the box being used. In order to keep the box in a true vertical position, layout with a level is recommended.*

Photo 107

STEP 2: *With a long auger-bit, drill a continuous vertical hole through the two rounds of logs; this eliminates misalignment of individually drilled holes.*

Electrical Installation

Photo 108

Photo 109

STEP 4: With a smaller drill, bore a series of holes near the perimeter of the box outline to the required depth, always adhering to the cutline.

STEP 3: A second hole is then drilled from the center of where the box will be, to connect with the vertical hole. AT THIS POINT CONSTRUCTION MAY CONTINUE, AND THE FOLLOWING STEPS DONE AFTER THE ROOF HAS BEEN COMPLETED.

The Handbook of Canadian Log Building

Photo 110

STEP 5: *The rectangular hole may now be chiselled to accommodate the box.*

Photo 111

STEP 6: *Note that the box used has an internal connector, and the wire must enter the bottom of the box near the back.*

Photo 112

STEP 7: *Another hole is drilled from the bottom of the electrical box hole to the initial vertical hole, at an angle of approximately 45 degrees.*

Electrical Installation

Photo 113

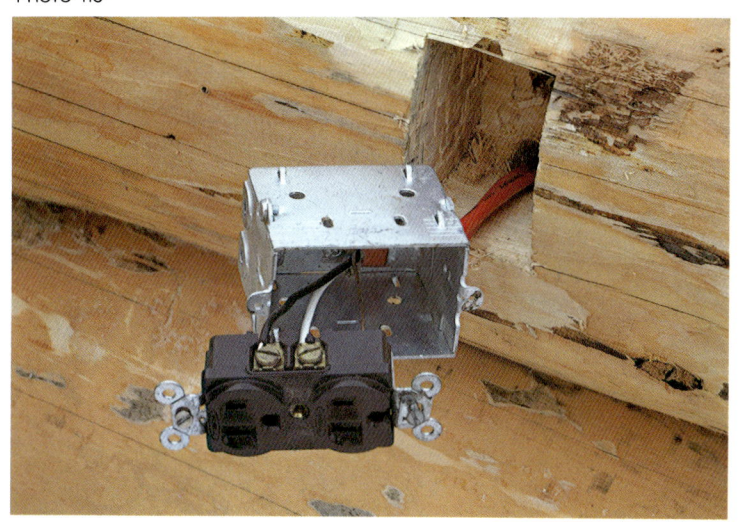

Photo 115

Photo 114

STEP 8: *The wire is now inserted up the vertical hole (from underneath the floor system) and through the electrical box, then attached to the electrical receptacle.*

STEP 9: *The electrical box is now fastened into the hole cut into the log. The sides of the log which protrude beyond the edges of the electrical box are bevelled to accommodate the receptacle cover.*

STEP 10: *The receptacle cover is put into place and the final touch-up of the bevelled faces is done.*

The Handbook of Canadian Log Building

Photo 116

Fig. 62

114

CHAPTER 15

Plumbing Installation

Whenever plumbing is incorporated into modern log construction, settling of the structure must be taken into account.

If the building is a single-storey bungalow then generally the only piping which the builder must be concerned with are the vent pipes and where they pass through the roof, as in Fig. 63. Once a multifloor structure is contemplated though, then plumbing becomes a major concern.

It is a good idea in any type of construction project to localize all the plumbing to one area of the building. Achieving this requires a designated area for vertical piping between floors. This is usually accomplished by either (1), constructing framed walls, one directly above the other, and locating the plumbing in the framework, or (2) building a small area in which much piping may be located. For the main piping where vertical movement of the piping is considered, a simple expansion coupling is used, as illustrated in Fig. 62. For the water lines, usually long horizontal runs, with soft walled piping, adequately allows for pipe deflection during the settling process.

The Handbook of Canadian Log Building

Photo 117

Plumbing Installation

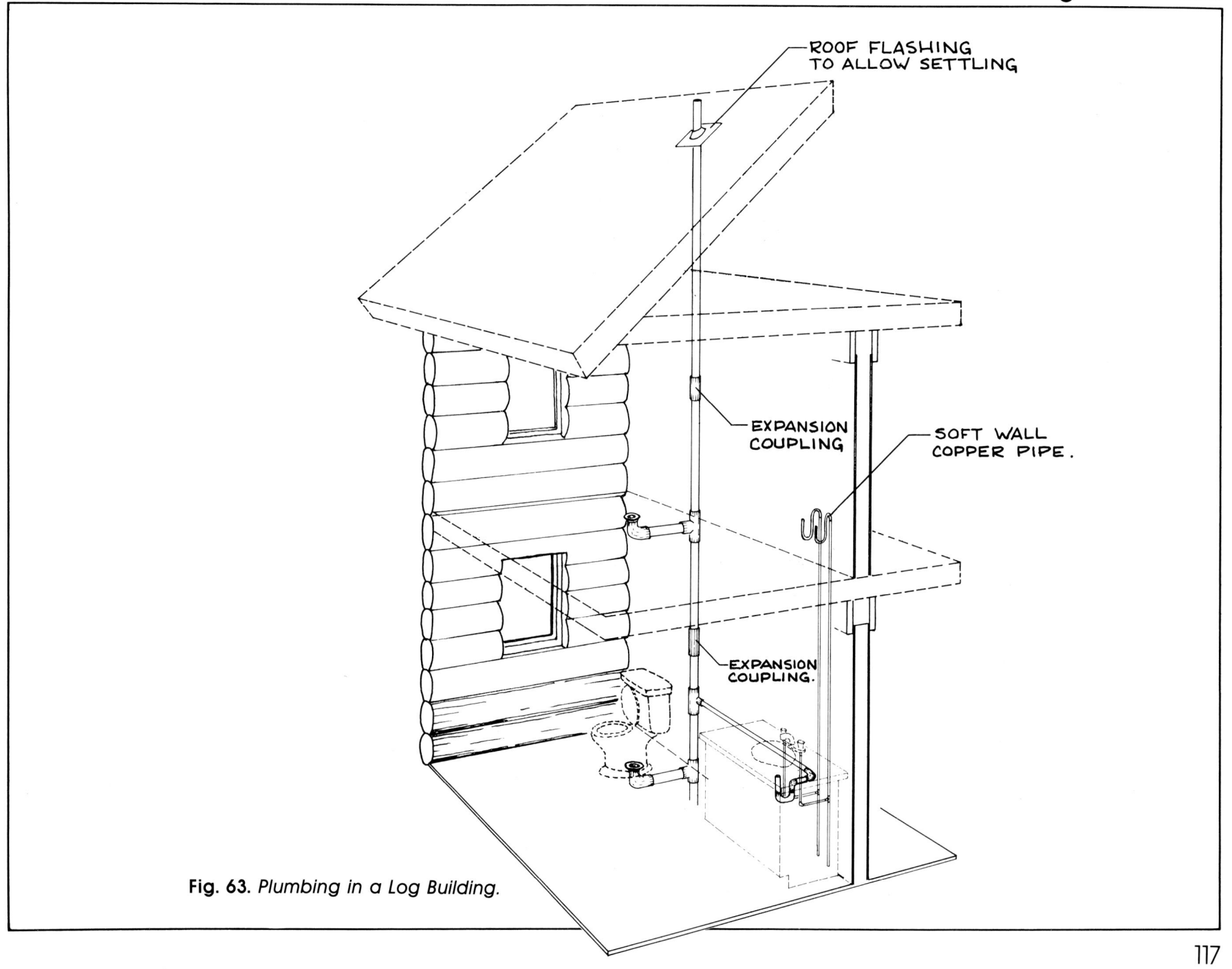

Fig. 63. *Plumbing in a Log Building.*

The Handbook of Canadian Log Building

Photo 118

CHAPTER 16

Stairs

Due to the settling which takes place in the early years of a new log building, a staircase must be constructed which will take this change into consideration.

There are many styles of staircases which may be used, but the two common types are the staircases constructed of half-log stringers and half-log treads, and the staircase built from half-log stringers and plank stairs with the planks covered with carpeting to match the building decor.

Because the second floor will move downward, the stringers must be able to actually "ski" along the floor during the settling process. In a 'straight-run' staircase very few problems are encountered, but when complicated stair designs are contemplated, a great deal of consideration must be given to settling or problems will arise later. *See Fig. 64.*

The Handbook of Canadian Log Building

Photo 120

Photo 122

Photo 119

Photo 121

120

Stairs

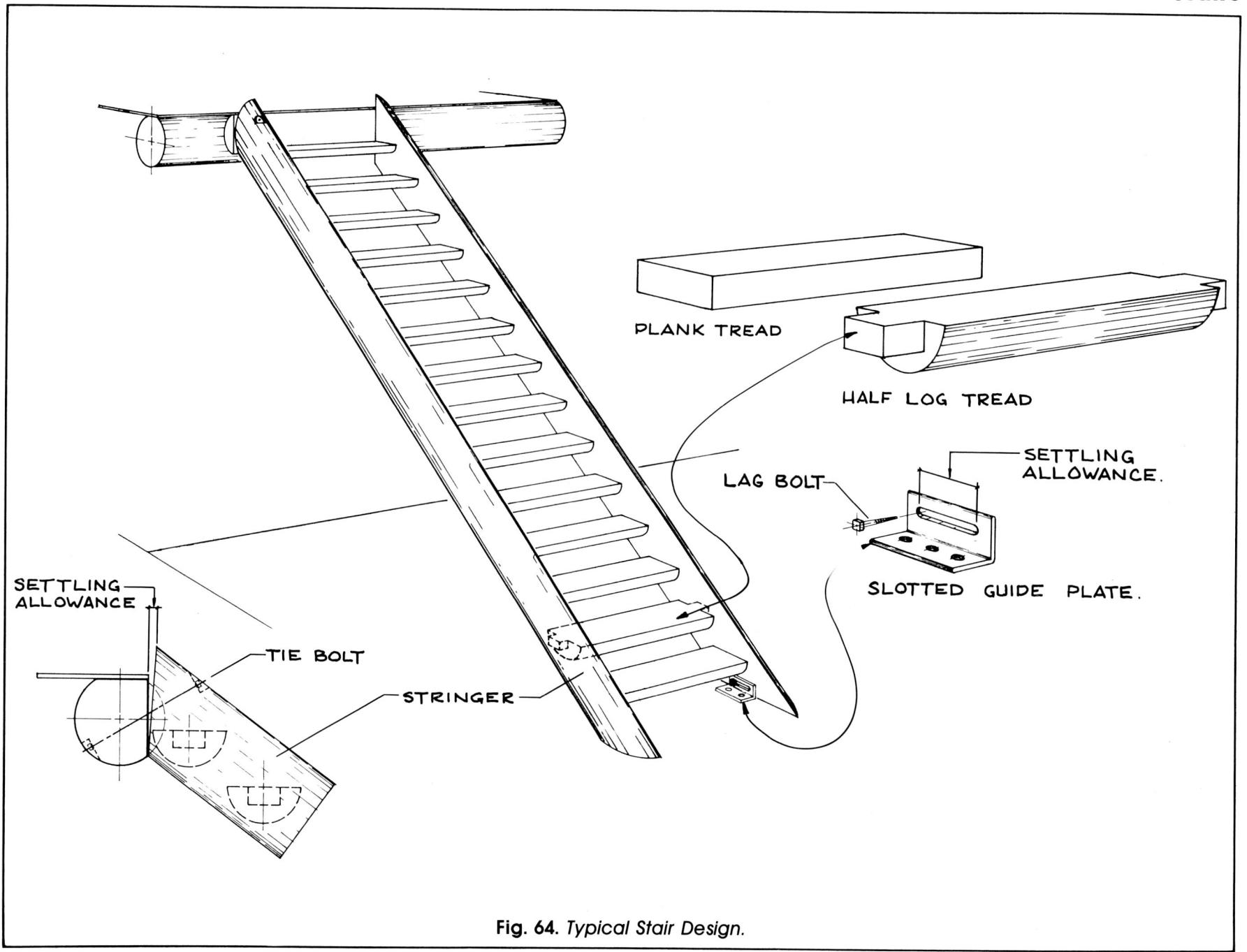

Fig. 64. *Typical Stair Design.*

121

The Handbook of Canadian Log Building

Photo 123

CHAPTER 17

Screw Jacks

In some cases, either for structural qualities or for aesthetic values, vertical supports are required in the construction of the log building. Since settling occurs throughout the building, consideration must be given to allow for adjustment of the vertical support which does not shrink or compress longitudinally (actually, in the case of log posts, shrinkage and compression does occur, but its amount is negligible). A widely used and accepted method of adjustment is by the use of a 'screw jack'. Basically, this is a mechanical device with an adjustable length, which is calculated using the settling formulas in Chapter 7. The 'screw jack' may be placed either at the bottom or the top of the vertical support, and access to the adjustment provided. In Fig. 64, the 'screw jack' is shown at the bottom of the support and after final settlement has occurred, a form may be built around the 'screw jack' cavity and filled with concrete. The use of a 'screw jack' on the interior of the building would require perhaps a cylindrical carpet sleeve to conceal the 'screw jack' cavity. The recommended minimum diameter for the 'screw jack shaft' is 7/8 inch (23 mm).

If, however, the 'screw jack' is placed at the top of the support, then usually a wooden skirting is provided around the 'screw jack cavity' to allow for the settling.

The Handbook of Canadian Log Building

Photo 124

Screw Jacks

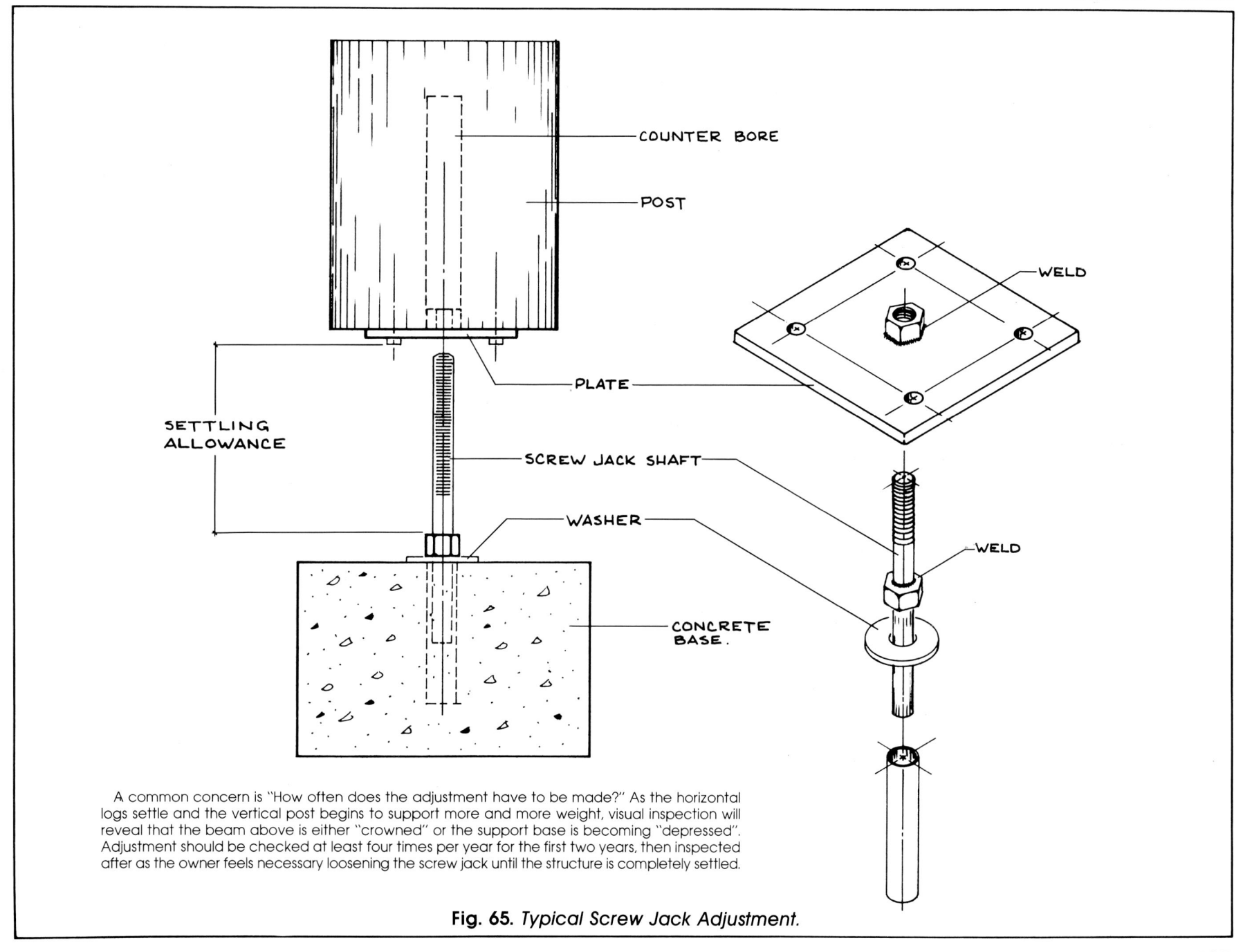

Labels (left diagram): COUNTER BORE, POST, PLATE, SETTLING ALLOWANCE, SCREW JACK SHAFT, WASHER, CONCRETE BASE.

Labels (right exploded view): WELD, WELD.

A common concern is "How often does the adjustment have to be made?" As the horizontal logs settle and the vertical post begins to support more and more weight, visual inspection will reveal that the beam above is either "crowned" or the support base is becoming "depressed". Adjustment should be checked at least four times per year for the first two years, then inspected after as the owner feels necessary loosening the screw jack until the structure is completely settled.

Fig. 65. *Typical Screw Jack Adjustment.*

125

CHAPTER 18

Trimming the Log Ends

Photo 125

The character of every building is determined by all the finishing touches and, certainly, by the shape of the log ends which extend beyond the notches. There are many different shapes which may be considered, and a few are shown in Fig. 66. In each case the building takes on a different appearance,

Trimming the Log Ends

quite likely depending on personal preference, building location and/or the feeling the structure is to convey.

It is advisable for the builder to keep two considerations in mind when working with the log ends. First, when scribing the log, the advanced builder certainly understands that widening the scribing distance for this portion of the log will greatly aid in the eventual settling of the logs. Because this portion of log is always at uniform temperature (there is no difference from inside-to-outside as there is along the main portion of the wall), the log reacts differently, settling at a slower rate than the remainder of the log.

Initially, the settling allowance between the logs might appear to indicate sloppy workmanship, or a novice builder, but this is not the case; rather, it is indicative of a well-built structure with forethought given to settling considerations.

The second consideration is that, when trimming the log ends, it's important to maintain adequate bearing beyond the notches to provide the necessary stability for the building. It's wise during construction to allow only about 2 inches (5 cm) for trimming; trimming too much off presents the danger of cutting into the lateral grooves. When trimming the log ends straight, a guide is recommended and also sighting from end to end will ensure that true cuts are made. See Fig. 68. Should a scroll or curved cut be desired a template is useful to achieve identical patterns throughout.

The Handbook of Canadian Log Building

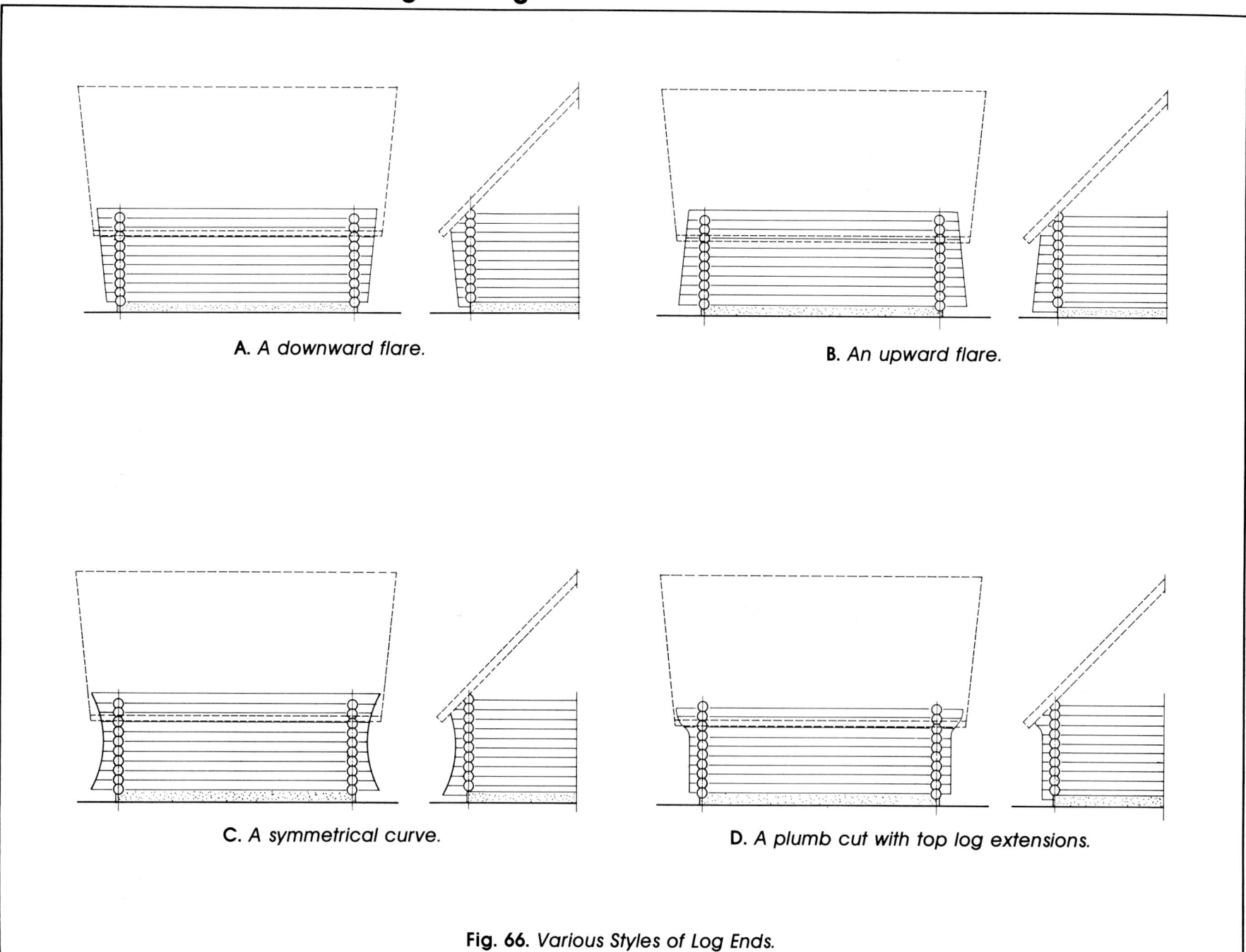

A. *A downward flare.*

B. *An upward flare.*

C. *A symmetrical curve.*

D. *A plumb cut with top log extensions.*

Fig. 66. *Various Styles of Log Ends.*

Trimming the Log Ends

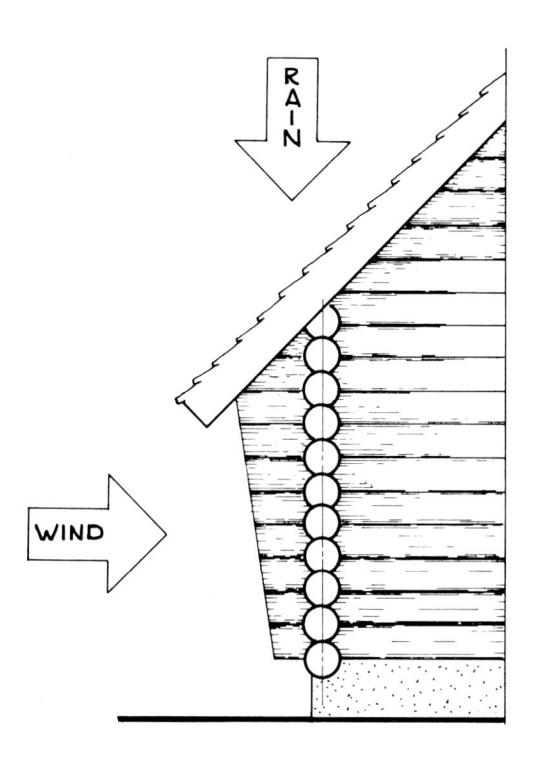

Fig. 67. *Adequate roof overhang protects the log ends from the elements.*

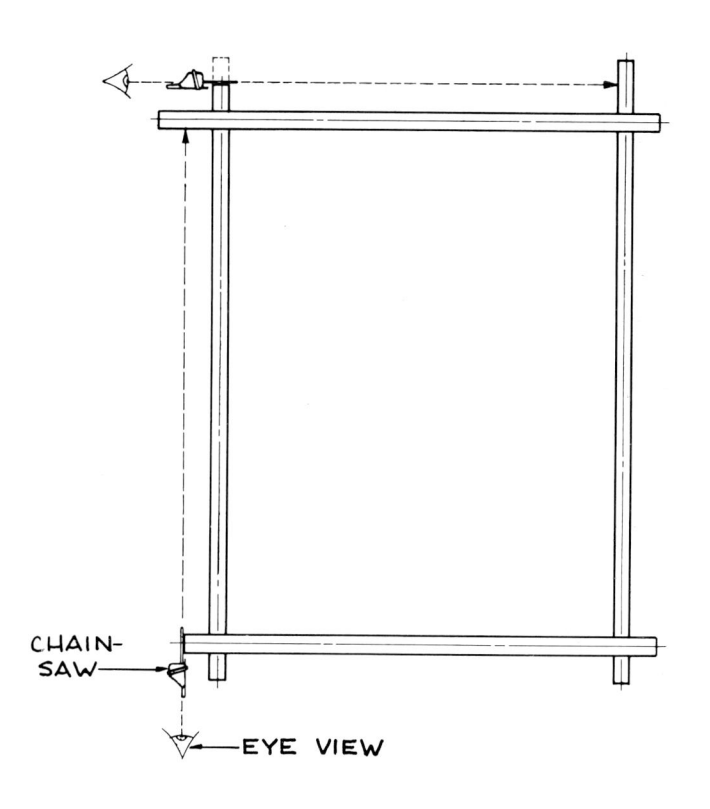

Fig. 68. *Sighting from end-to-end for accurate cutting.*

As many old log buildings show, rotting is possible at the log ends. Any small crevice or check in the log ends is at the mercy of the elements if there is inadequate roof overhang or if prevailing winds continually drive moisture against the logs. See Fig. 67.

The Handbook of Canadian Log Building

Photo 126

130

CHAPTER 19

Wood Preservation

Log structures are noted for their longevity; they are capable of lasting for hundreds of years with minimal attention. But the relics dotting some North American landscapes, while still standing, aren't prime examples of what most log builders visualize when they begin their work. The fact is that careful thought must be given to how best to preserve and protect the logs being used. To understand what must be done, it is best to also understand the peculiarities of logs as a building form.

Unlike trees grown in bygone years, modern timber tends to be planted in fast-growing open stands which produce more sapwood than durable, resistant heartwood, so the need to protect logs from insect attack and decay has also increased. One of the most important factors a builder should consider is that resistance of logs to insects, stain or decay depends on the time of year the timber is cut. Spring and summer-cut logs will experience difficulty with mildew, sapstain and insect infestation; because this is the time of year when the sap is flowing, such trees will peel more easily but check worse than those felled duing the dormant season in fall and winter.

The Handbook of Canadian Log Building

Builders using fresh logs should be aware that sapwood is menaced by three living organisms: molds, insects and fungi. The molds cause only superficial discoloration and can be easily removed through brushing, sanding or shallow planing of the wood surface. Not so with the fungi (typically brown-rot or white-rot), which pose a greater threat, often without any outwardly visible signs. The presence of fungi indicates that some sort of wood preservative treatment is needed. One simple precaution is to remember that although spores from infected wood can be carried by the wind to germinate in sound logs with more than a 20 per cent moisture content, dry wood doesn't allow the spores to grow and so won't decay.

It is most important that the builder realizes that the growth of stains (molds) and decay (fungi) are dependent on three very crucial conditions; (1) ideal temperature, (2) the moisture content, and (3) the presence of food (sugars contained in the sap).

Perhaps the greatest threat facing the growth of stains (molds) and decay (fungi) comes from the continual cycles of wetting and drying. Since drying logs shrink mostly diametrically and very little longitudinally, checking can't be avoided; it may be reduced in well-seasoned timber but it can never be eliminated. And even minute checks will open fresh, untreated wood to insects and decay.

As if this isn't enough, the sun's ultra-violet rays interact with the acid in the wood to take their toll

Wood Preservation

on the building's exterior.

The single most important factor in keeping logs new and healthy-looking is regular maintenance. This should begin during the construction phase with preventative building techniques designed to keep the log deck as well as the structure as dry as possible while at the same time discouraging insects. It's rather difficult to keep an entire log deck dry, however, by making sure that each log has ventilation around it completely (ie. the logs are off the ground and not touching one another), and by turning the logs 180 degrees often to allow for drying, partial control of the mold and fungi attack may be achieved. The builder should be aware of the fact that the time required for fungi and mold to spread throughout an entire "set" of building logs is measured in a "few days" or even perhaps "hours", if the right conditions are present. Should the occasion arise to apply a chemical preservative to the logs, it must be done, not at the builder's convenience, but rather before moisture, or the humidity, has a chance to work with the living organisms and cause them to spread.

Ventilation beneath the floor is important to keep the ground under the building dry; no matter what foundation is used, proper air circulation is essential. Another factor in keeping the building dry is any design which accelerates rainwater run-off. The landscape surrounding the building should be

The Handbook of Canadian Log Building

sloped steeply away, and perhaps some water-absorbing shrubs planted nearby. Builders should also ensure that any logs used with checks or cracks are placed in a facedown position. Remember too, that any treatment of "green" or partially-seasoned logs, with the exception of pressure treatment, has little lasting value.

A finish on the interior and exterior of the log surfaces completes the process of guarding against decay. The interior finish should be designed simply to provide for ease of cleaning while enhancing the natural color and beauty of the logs. Exterior finishes are many and varied, each with advantages and problems inherent in their use. When choosing a finish for the exterior of a log structure, consider the effectiveness of the preservation itself, whether it will blister or peel later on, whether it allows the wood underneath to breathe, and finally, how it will affect the natural appearance of the structure.

It is not the intent of this book to recommend a suitable preservative, however, regardless of what type is used (and there are several reputable ones on the market to choose from) it will only be effective if a regular maintenance program is followed. There is no such thing as a maintenance-free finish and no natural product lasts forever, but a properly cared-for log building will continue to be a thing of beauty for many, many years.

Wood Preservation

Photo 127

The Handbook of Canadian Log Building

Photo 128

CHAPTER 20

Timeless Love — Man's Attraction to Log Building

Trees are one of our oldest natural resources and for years their appeal lay in the fact that the supply was renewable and therefore never-ending. Recently mankind has become aware that nothing – not even a resource as seemingly unlimited as our forests – lasts forever. This has brought about an increased awareness of the value of our forest resources and the need for proper management of them, but although we are beginning to realize we must be careful how we use our trees, this only enhances our appreciation of one of the oldest forms of construction – log building.

The human race has had a love affair with homes and other buildings made from trees for centuries – almost from the time caves became too damp and clay homes lost their appeal. While log building is admittedly enjoying a resurgence in

The Handbook of Canadian Log Building

today's society, its historical roots go back much further.

What may be the first recorded reference to log home construction involves horizontal timbering (pyramid-style) on the Black Sea shore in 30 B.C. While this form of log construction never achieved widespread popularity, there are similar references to vertical timbering in Anglo-Saxon England in 1015, and this building style has stayed with us, albeit with many variations, until the present day.

The concept of log construction was, from the first, admirably suited to North America with its seemingly endless supply of trees. This fact was appreciated by the Swedish settlers who moved to Delaware Bay, Pennsylvania in 1638, and built New Sweden using traditional techniques and the trees they found everywhere around them in their new habitat. Germans from Bavaria added their techniques to those of the Swedes when they settled the area around 1710.

The log building concept that really took hold, though, resulted from the migration of the adventuresome Scotch-Irish to the western lands in the 1720's. The ever-practical Irish seized this building form as the quickest, cheapest and easiest form of construction available to them, and it soon became a trademark of western living.

Timeless Love — Man's Attraction to Log Building

In the 19th century, at least in the eastern and southern parts of North America, logs were fashionably covered with siding and by the end of the century sawn wood, bricks and stone began replacing logs as the major sources of home building materials.

But the log homes, churches, mills and other structures didn't disappear from the landscape; they outlived many of their competitors and made a reappearance in the form of rustic-styled buildings in the 1920's and 30's. Ten years later the fad of rustic building began petering out, but log building in general continued, mostly in the form of vacation homes.

At the present time log building is enjoying its greatest popularity in years. It has evolved recently from the early, primitive cabin concept to the ultimate in present-day, good-quality construction. While most modern structures don't approach the size of the Log Chateau at Montebello, Quebec (the largest log structure in the world), they have become a statement of the rugged individualist, a philosophical statement about the values of the pure, simple life. Nowadays the designs are as varied and personalized as the designers and builders themselves, for log building permits an

The Handbook of Canadian Log Building

exceptional amount of personalization by the builder, perhaps more than any conventional form of construction.

Nearly everyone who builds a log structure or contemplates doing so gives some thought to the timeless attraction of this construction method. Log buildings are, of course, natural solutions to structural problems. They are very old and have been found in many parts of the world, yet throughout history little interest has been evinced by architectural historians in this building method. They seemed to think it was merely functional and built to be abandoned. Yet log building has persevered, and some of these buildings are in use today, 1,400 years after they were constructed.

There is no doubt that log homes were originally appealing because they were easy to assemble, economical, and needed only simple, periodic care. In the difficult years of settlement a man could build his own house, barn and out-buildings – from logs cut in the land-clearing operation. But despite these humble beginnings, log homes have traditionally retained their beauty even when suffering the onslaught of time, neglect and abandonment. With the advancement of techniques used by modern day builders, along with proper care, they could – and in some cases likely will – last for a thousand years.

Glossary of Building Terms

ANCHOR BOLT: usually a steel pin which is embedded in concrete to which the sill plate is anchored. P. 3, 146.

BEAM: a horizontal timber framing member.

BEARING: a term used which refers to the amount of contact between two surfaces for an adequate connection.

BUTTS: the large end of a log. P. 61.

CHECKING: the splitting apart of the wood cells caused by rapid drying.

COUNTERFLASHING: a flashing which when applied over the regular flashing, allows for movement between the two flashings and still provides a weathertight seal. P. 105.

COVE: a shallow groove with a profile which is a rounded shape, on the underside of a log. P. 51.

CRITICAL POINTS: during the layout of the Double-Scribe Notch, these are the points created by the intersection of a level line through the scribe line. P. 5, 21, 22.

DEAD-LOAD: the weight applied to a structural member due to the sum of the weights of **only the material** which it is supporting.

DECK: a term which refers to the pile of logs which are to be used during construction; also a building term for an exposed balcony.

DORMER: framing which is attached to, and projects from the roof and allows for extra headroom and light for the usable area contained within the sloping area of the roof. P. 65.

DRIFT PIN: a pin attaching two or more members together; slightly larger in diameter than the pilot hole so that a snug fit is obtained. P. 61, 75, 77.

EAVE: the overhang of the roof which projects beyond the walls.

FACIA: a trim board usually covering the exposed ends of the rafters. P. 146.

The Handbook of Canadian Log Building

FLASHING: a weatherproof stripping which when attached to the building is capable of shedding moisture from vital areas. P. 3, 105, 146.

FOOTING: the base which is directly beneath the foundation wall and supports the structure above; the width of the footing is usually wider than the foundation wall; the size and type of footings are dependent on the design of the structure and the soil conditions. P. 3, 27, 146.

FOUNDATION: that part of the structure which is usually beneath the grade and supports the entire weight of the building. P. 3, 27, 146.

GABLE: the upper portion of the end wall which is usually triangular shaped; also a term referring to the exposed ends of the cabinets. P. 69, 102, 103.

GRADE: a term which means the finished height of the soil surrounding the building. P. 146.

INSULATION: material designed to impede the transfer of heat through the outer surfaces of the living areas of the house. P. 92, 146.

JOIST: horizontal load bearing members; usually supporting floor, ceiling or roof. P. 3, 19, 146.

KEY: see SPLINE.

KERF: a term used to refer to the width of wood being removed by the thickness of the saw blade when cutting.

KICKBACK: a force which opposes the direction of the chainsaw chain, and when this force becomes greater than the directional force of the chain, causes the chainsaw to be forced in the direction of the operator and may result in serious injury.

LAG BOLT: a bolt which resembles an ordinary bolt with the only difference being that a wood screw type thread replaces the familiar machine thread. P. 99, 121.

LATERAL GROOVE: a continuous groove with cross-section which is either a rounded shape or a "V" shape on the underside of the log. P. 53.

LIVE LOAD: a measure of external forces acting on structural members; usually in terms of snow load, wind load or domestic traffic.

LEVEL: in a true horizontal position.

MORTISE: a square or rectangular hole cut into a log or beam to allow a tenon to be inserted.

Glossary of Building Terms

NAILER:	wooden stock attached to the logwork for settling precautions and to which the appropriate pieces of construction (partition, kitchen cabinet, etc.) can be secured while still allowing the logwork to settle. P. 92, 93, 103.
NOTCH – BLIND:	a notch which does not extend completely through the timber with which it is mated. P. 29.
– DOUBLE-SCRIBED:	also called LOCKING NOTCH or SQUARE NOTCH; a notch whose exterior appearance is identical to that of the round notch but whose interior is composed of an interlocking square lap; with this notch both logs are scribed to fit the contour of the other. P. 18-25.
– ROUND:	on the underside of each log, a notch with a semicircular shape, is removed to fit over the log below. P. 31-57.
OUTRIGGER BEAM:	A log which rests on top of cantilevered logs from the gable walls and is parallel to and out beyond the plate logs. To this beam the roof framing is attached. P. 67.
PLATE LOG:	the top wall log on the building. P. 69, 71, 75, 76, 79, 83, 146.
PLUMB:	in a true vertical position. P. 7.
POST:	A vertical timber framing member. P. 125.
PURLIN:	a roof supporting beam, usually placed in line between the plate log and the ridge-pole. P. 69, 75, 76, 79, 83, 146.
RAFTER:	pieces of dimensional lumber which support (a) the roofing material and (b) the live loads applied to the roof.
RECURVE:	when the shape of a notch is **more** than a half-circle, then the log to which it is being scribed is said to be in a "recurve" situation.
RIDGE-POLE:	a roof-supporting beam which is placed at the peak of the roof. P. 69, 75, 76, 79, 83, 146.
ROOF-JOIST:	pieces of dimensional lumber which support (a) the roofing material, (b) the live loads applied to the roof, and (c) the ceiling material. P. 69, 146.
SCRIBER:	a device to accurately transfer the shape of one piece of material to the surface of another. P. 30.

The Handbook of Canadian Log Building

SCRIBING: the process of transfering the shape of one piece of material to the surface of another. P. 31-57.

SCREW-JACK: a mechanical device which may be adjusted to allow for the difference in height between horizontally fitted logs and the support timber caused by settling. P. 122-125.

SETTLING: the vertical movement of the logs due to the combination of the natural shrinkage of the material and the compression of the wood fibers. P. 58-59.

SILL – LOG: the bottom log in the wall. P. 146.

    – WINDOW: the bottom of the window. P. 93.

    – PLATE: a piece of dimensional lumber which is connected to the foundation wall by anchor bolts. The structure of the building is then built above this. P. 3, 27, 146.

SKIRTING: a facia-type material at the top of the window, door or partition opening; it is fastened in such a manner as to allow for the settling of the logs. P. 92, 93, 98, 99.

SOFFIT: the underside of the roof overhang. P. 146.

SPLINE: a piece of material, usually wood or metal, inserted into the ends of the logs after an opening has been cut through the log wall; used to stabilize the structure. P. 92, 93.

STAIR STRINGER: that part of the stairs which supports the treads. P. 121.

STAIR TREADS: that part, which when walking on the stairs, the feet make contact with. P. 121.

TEMPLATE: a piece of material, such as plywood, used as a tracing device with the shape of the desired pattern.

TENON: a square of rectangular form on the end of a log, or timber, which is inserted into a mortise. P. 77, 83, 69.

TRUSS: the arrangement of timbers such that the constructed form will support (a) its own weight, plus (b) the calculated extraneous forces acting on it. P. 73, 75, 76, 77.

VAPOUR BARRIER: material which is capable of preventing the transfer of moisture. P. 3, 146.

V-GROOVE: see LATERAL GROOVE.

WEDGES: tapered pieces of material used to pre-stress logs in order to localize the checking; also used to apply tension for a splice-type of joinery. P. 61.

Glossary of Building Terms

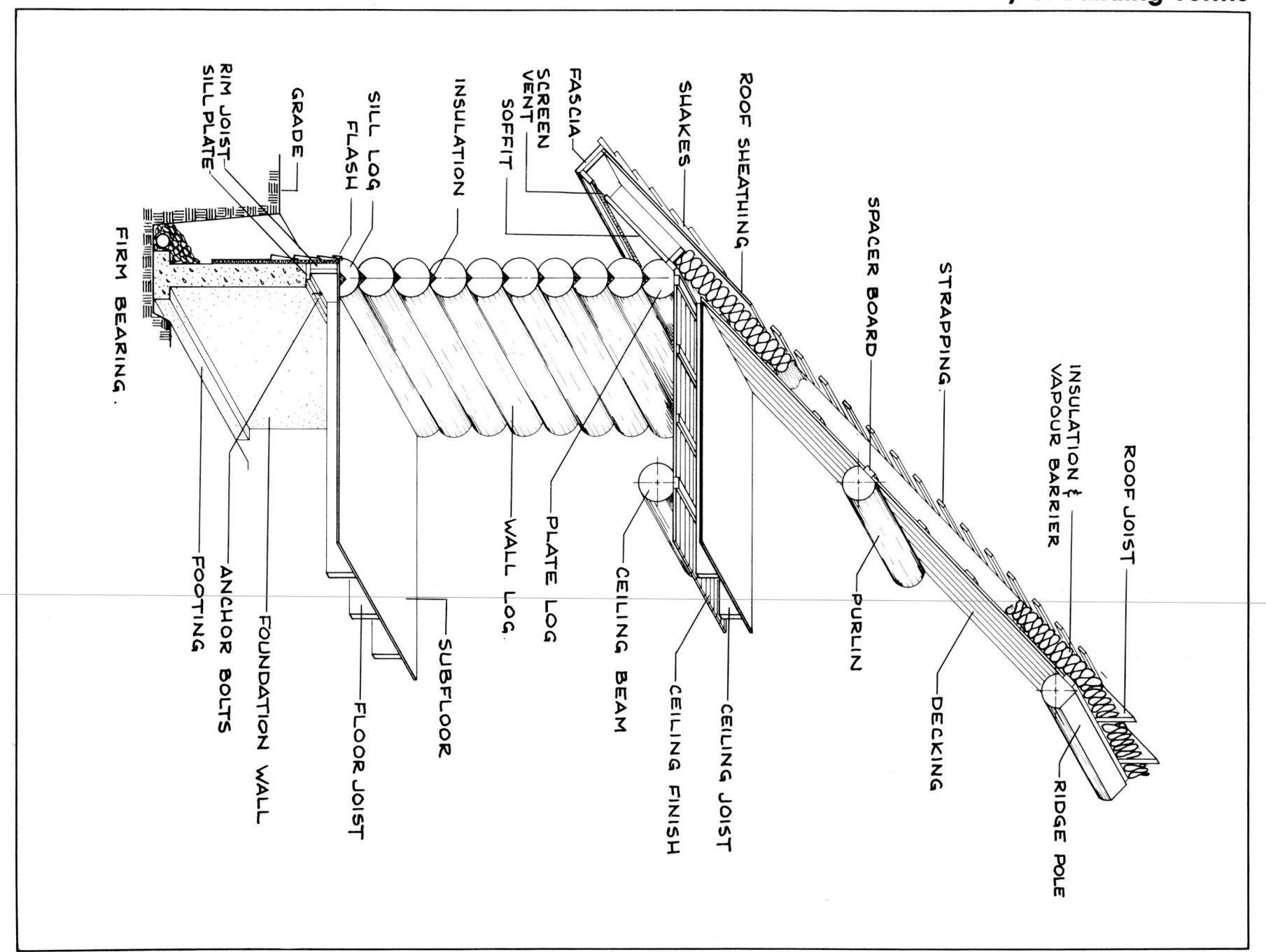

About the Author

F. Dan Milne (1954-   ), the son of Edward and Doreen Milne, was born and raised in Pritchard, British Columbia, Canada. His father was a logger and farmer, and the love to work with wood and nature has been a harmonious part of his life as long as he can remember. After graduating from high school and attending college on a science and mathematics program, Dan decided that his niche in life should be a hands-on environment, working with materials that he was familiar with – wood. Through sheer luck, he became aware of a log building construction course in Prince George, British Columbia, taught by B. Allan Mackie. In 1974 he immediately enrolled in the program. Since that initial course, Dan has worked on numerous log building projects and has taught many log house building courses throughout western Canada. A unique opportunity arose when Dan was invited to Japan in 1983 to conduct log building courses, and thus sparked the dream of this book – a reference manual to aid builders, authorities and homeowners and to guide them through some of the topics unique to the log building industry.

Also available through the Log Home Guide for Builders & Buyers

BUILDING WITH LOGS, by B. Allan Mackie. The indispensable textbook for anyone even remotely interested in log building. Profusely illustrated and written by a man deeply committed to handcrafted log buildings. A standard textbook in most log building courses. 76 pps. Hardcover $25.00; softcover $16.

NOTCHES OF ALL KINDS, by B. Allan Mackie. Master log builder Mackie describes all the notches and joints used in log construction with an explanation of the special function of each. Lavishly illustrated with step-by-step diagrams and photographs. Like Mackie's other books, a must for the serious log builder. 90 pps. $16.

LOG HOUSE PLANS, by Allan Mackie. The latest book by the guru of handcrafted log builders. 37 complete Mackie house plans and an excellent introduction giving recommendations for a Survival Lifestyle. Appendices on construction, finishing and preserving. A must for every builder and buyer. 172 pps. Softcover $16.

THE TIMBER FRAMING BOOK, by S. Elliott & E. Wallas. A must for anyone interested in timberframe structure. Profusely illustrated with accurate professional drawings and dozens of on-the-job action photographs. 169 pp. $13.95 ($15.95 in Canada).

LOG BUILDING TOOLS & HOW TO MAKE THEM, by R. D. Arcand. Do it yourself and save hundreds of dollars. A guide and inspiration to those with the inclination to make their own tools. Describes many tools which are hard to find today. Profusely illustrated. 64 pps $6.95.

LOG STRUCTURES: PRESERVATION AND PROBLEM-SOLVING, by Harrison Goodall and Renee Friedman. Practical, detailed instructions for dealing with the difficulties in log constructions — wood decay, loose chinking, leaking roofs and sagging floors. Chapters cite measures for salvaging, and provide guidance in planning restoration with specific techniques for preserving. Some 93 photographs and 57 diagrams illustrate how to accomplish each step. With this book, new life is assured to thousands of historic log structures urgently in need of rescue – and healthier life to their modern counterparts. 119 pages. $10.95 ($12.95 in Canada).

THE COMPLETE LOG HOUSE BOOK, by Dale Mann and Richard Skinulis. Photography by Nancy Shanoff. A beautifully illustrated and inspiring book covering all aspects of design and construction of the four methods of log building: hewn, long log, piece-on-piece and stackwall. Valuable information on planning, materials, tools, techniques, insulation, wood preservatives, and much more. An essential textbook for all builders. 176 pps. $12.95 ($14.95 in Canada).

BUILDING THE TIMBER FRAME HOUSE, by Ted Benson with James Gruber. Illustrations by Jamie Page. Written by the owner of a post-and-beam construction firm in New Hampshire and a civil engineer, this book tells exactly how to build a timber frame house. Beginning with a brief, interesting chapter on the history of timber framing, the authors include chapters on the kinds of joinery, the assembly of timbers and raising. The last part of the book deals with present-day design and materials: house plans, site development, foundation-laying, insulation, tools and methods. $13.95 ($16.95 in Canada).

THE ENERGY ECONOMICS AND THERMAL PERFORMANCE OF LOG HOUSES, by Muir-Osborne. For years, the *Log Home Guide for Builders & Buyers* has been gathering data and supporting research on the energy-efficiency of log homes. This material now confirms the superiority of the log home and it's documented in this book written by the *Log Home Guide*'s editorial staff. $5.

YOUR LOG HOUSE, by Vic Janzen. The most comprehensive textbook yet written on how to build your own log house. With frequent references to a simple house plan, master craftsman Vic Janzen follows a step-by-step, cumulative approach to building. Janzen is careful to spell out possible problems and to caution first-time builders about any delusions or preconceived notions they may bring to a project. Interior stud wall framing, electrical work, heating, mathematics of roof building, use of subtrades, are also dealt with. 169 pps., 140 + line drawings and almost as many photographs. $15.00.

BUILDING THE ALASKA LOG HOME, Tom Walker. "I doubt there is another book in the market that would inspire one to build like this one does. The photography, all of it in color, is superb. Walker includes many examples of appealing buildings in a great variety of designs, from the trappers cabin to the elegant log home in suburbia. The design principles articulate the excellence. Walker's love for his work shines through. If his buildings are as handcrafted as his book, he is a man to be admired. This book is certainly a welcome addition to my building library and I am pleased to recommend it." – Vic Janzen, author of 'Your Log House'. 178 pages. Softcover $19.95 ($23.95 Can.)

BEFORE YOU BUILD: A PRECONSTRUCTION GUIDE, Robert Roskind. This book is a must for those planning to build their own log home or any home for that matter. Using a checklist/questionnaire format, Roskind outlines what questions need to be answered and helps the do-it-yourselfer organize his construction schedule in the most efficient way. The book asks questions such as, "Is there good southern exposure for passive or active solar use? What is the zoning on the land? Does the land welcome you?" Instead of thinking "Hmm... I should have thought of that earlier" when a problem crops up, this volume will help the owner/builder avoid potential pitfalls. 149 pp., checklists and illustrations. Softcover $7.95 (Can. $8.95).

STAV OG LAFT I NORGE, Early Wooden Architecture in Norway, Gunnar Bugge and Christian Norberg-Schultz. The first comprehensive work on the folk-architecture of Norway. The authors have selected about 60 representative examples illustrating the different types of farms, farm houses and stave-churches, and have treated the historical and artistic development in a general introduction. The book has 168 large pages and over 400 illustrations. Text is in Norwegian and English. Hardcover $27.50 ($35.00 Can.)

THE CRAFT OF LOG BUILDING, Hermann Phleps. Now translated from the German, this outstanding book is the most important volume on log building available in the northern hemisphere. A classic in Germany *The Craft of Log Building* is the master work of Hermann Phleps, whose career as an architect and teacher of the art of timber-work spanned nearly 60 years. *The Craft of Log Building* includes 419 drawings and photographs. Some of Phleps' examples of wood craftsmanship far exceed the purely ornamental and can only be described as exceptional artistry. 328 pp., 11" by 8-1/2" Softcover $19.95.

THE BOOK OF MASONRY STOVES, David Lyle. The masonry stove, widely used in Europe and Asia for centuries, surmounts many of the serious problems associated with wood heat and iron stoves: chimney fires, air pollution, poor energy efficiency. *The Book of Masonry Stoves* is the first comprehensive survey of all the major types of masonry heating systems, ancient and modern. Detailed plans and building information are included in the book. "Readers will find it hard to leave the book without having an overwhelming desire to install one of these wonderfully efficient, sensible devices in their home," writes Richard Ketchum, editor of Blair & Ketchum's *Country Journal.* 192 pages. Full of illustrations. Softcover $14.95 ($18.75 Can.)

HOW TO AFFORD YOUR OWN LOG HOME, Carl Heldmann. This book explains how you can build your own log home and save a lot of money by acting as your own contractor. Each step in the building process is examined, together with pitfalls, so that you can surmount the problems on your own. We feel it is an indispensable guide for the beginning builder who needs instructions about the Who, What, Why, When, Where and How of dealing with local tradesmen, building officials, banks and the whole complicated subject of erecting a house. We wish it had been in print before we started building! 137 pages, many photographs, charts, forms, etc. Softcover $9.95 ($12.95 Can.)

LOG HOME DESIGN, by the editorial staff of *Log Home Guide* magazine. Forty-seven log house plans representing various design trends, also feature articles on how to design a log home, environmental design, and traditional principles and contemporary design. $3.00.

Readers interested in any of these titles may obtain further information from the Log Home Guide Mail Order Book-Log, Muir Publishing Co. Ltd., Gardenvale, Que., Canada H9X 1B0, (or) Muir Publishing Co. Ltd., P.O. Box 1150, Plattsburgh, NY 12901. Credit card users may call toll-free: 1-800-345-LOGS (USA), 1-800-624-7214 (TENNESSEE); in Canada (514) 457-2045.

For more information about log homes, write or phone: Log Home Guide Information Center, Exit 447, I-40, Hartford, TN 37753. (615) 487-2256.

- Exhibition Hall
- Research Library
- Book Store
- LHG editorial office
- International Registry of Log Homes

A Japanese edition of
The Handbook of Canadian Log Building
is available through:
Yamakei Publishing Company Limited
1-1-33 Shiba Daimon Minapo-Ku
Tokyo 105, Japan
(Telephone: 03-436-4021)